Winkley Family

The
English Origin
of
Captain
Samuel Winkley
and Some
New England Descendants

William Haslet Jones

HERITAGE BOOKS
2016

HERITAGE BOOKS

AN IMPRINT OF HERITAGE BOOKS, INC.

Books, CDs, and more—Worldwide

For our listing of thousands of titles see our website
at
www.HeritageBooks.com

Published 2016 by
HERITAGE BOOKS, INC.
Publishing Division
5810 Ruatan Street
Berwyn Heights, Md. 20740

International Standard Book Numbers
Paperbound: 978-0-7884-1022-2
Clothbound: 978-0-7884-6321-1

WINKLEY FAMILY

TABLE OF CONTENTS

WINKLEY FAMILY

WINKLEY FAMILY

INTRODUCTION

Capt. Samuel WINKLEY, mariner, was the earliest WINKLEY ancestor to settle in New England. Reportedly he arrived at Portsmouth, NH on 9 Aug. 1680. [Fred Drew WINKLEY] Tradition says he came from Co. Lancashire, England. [Amer. Ancestry] Some claim he was born at Clitheroe in 1660, but offer no proof. [Lillian WINKLEY Jersh] Tradition proved to be wrong. Samuel was baptized at Dawlish, Co. Devonshire on 1 Oct. 1660 the son of Nicholas WINKLEY. Dawlish is a seaport on the English Channel at the mouth of the River Exe, near Exeter, England.

Prior to the arrival of Samuel WINKLEY in 1680, by some 17 years, the name of Nicholas WINKLEY is briefly found at Portsmouth, NH. He witnessed the 1662/3 will of Richard Seward. Richard Seward was a prominent ship owner, boat builder and exporter of tobacco. The name of Nicholas WINKLEY does not appear in any other New England records for this period. The names of the other three witnesses of Richard Seward's will, likewise do not appear elsewhere in New England records. Perhaps Nicholas WINKLEY was associated with the Sewards through their shipping business. He might even have been the capt. of their ship "Properouse." Reportedly Richard Seward came from the Exeter area of Co. Devon. Proof that this Nicholas WINKLEY was the same one living in Dawlish Co. Devon was found. Samuel was definitely his son.

Review of the parish records of St. Gregory, Dawlish indicated that the Winkleys first appeared there by 1543 [Devon Lay Subsidy Roll of 1543] Nicholas was born c1610. He married Mary Headon d/o Richard Headon, master mariner in 1632. He was the father of Samuel bp 1 Oct. 1660. The last WINKLEY entry at Dawlish St. Gregory appeared in 1732. It does not appear that the Winkleys came from Co. Lancashire. The basis for that tradition is apparently incorrect.

WINKLEY FAMILY

The name of WINKLEY in county Devon can be traced back to as early as 1219, and at Exeter to 1228. A **MICHAEL WYNKELEY** was at Budleigh in 1273. This is close to the site of WINKLEY MANOR found in the 16th century. No doubt early names of "de Wynkeley" reflect that they came from the north Devon parish of Winckleigh. See page 23 for a complete list of medieval WINKLEY names.

The author wishes to acknowledge the significant contribution made by Mr. Michael J.L. Wickes, of Bideford, Co. Devon, England. He has been a member of Association of Genealogists and Record Agents [AGRA] since 1981. He conducted research at the Devon Record Office and at Dawlish on the WINKLEY name.

This book is dedicated to my maternal Grandmother Evelyn May WINKLEY 1872-1916.

EVELYN MAY WINKLEY

MAP OF ENGLAND

Winkley Hall

London

Winkley Manor

Exeter

Dawlish

Location of the Parish of Dawlish County, Devonshire, England.

WINKLEY FAMILY

ABBREVIATIONS

Admin. = Administrator

b.   = born

c   = circa = about

ch.   = children

d.   = died

div.   = divorced

d/o   = daughter of

d.s.p. = died single person

d.y.   = died young

J.P.   = Justice of the Peace

md.   = married

m.1,   = married first

m.2,   = married second, etc.

P.P.   = personal property

Res.   = resident

s/o   = son of

unmd.   = unmarried

w/o   = wife of or widow of

PART 1

WINKLEY FAMILY - ENGLAND

1543 - 1700

WINKLEY FAMILY - ENGLAND

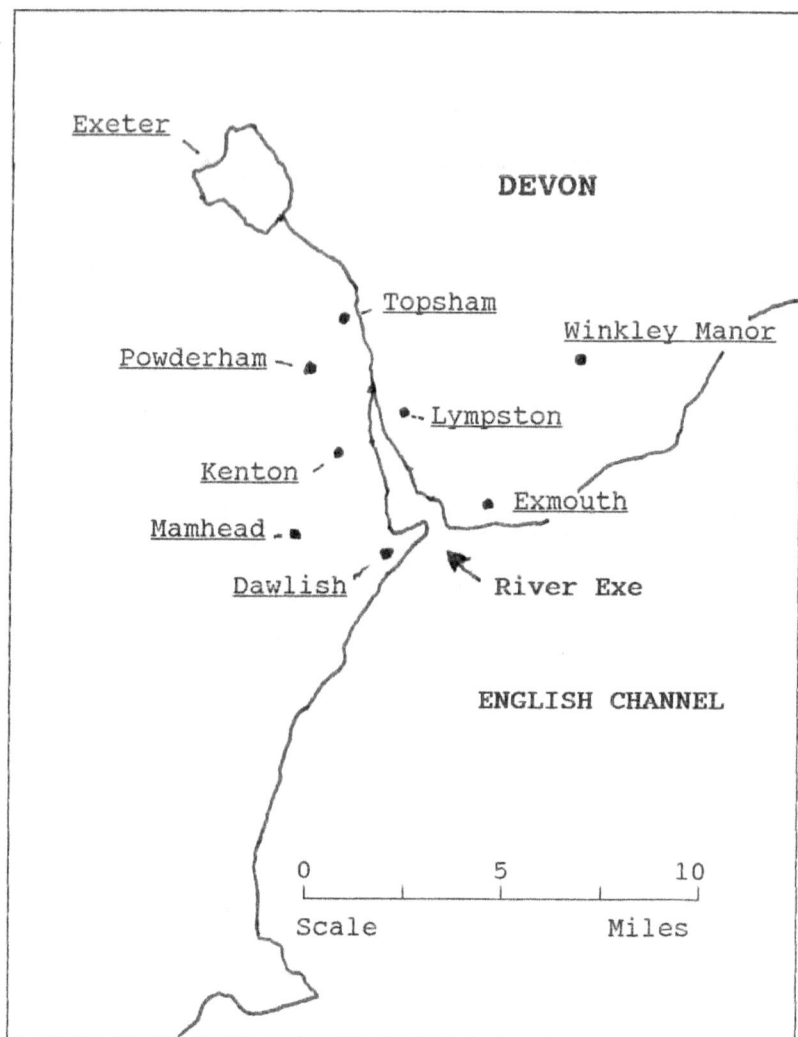

Exeter

DEVON

Topsham

Winkley Manor

Powderham

Lympston

Kenton

Exmouth

Mamhead

Dawlish

River Exe

ENGLISH CHANNEL

```
0              5             10
|---|---|---|---|---|---|---|---|
Scale                    Miles
```

BACKGROUND:

Tradition says that Capt. Samuel WINKLEY was born about 1660 in Co, Lancashire possibly at Clitheroe. [Lillian Winkley Jersh] But she offers no proof. A review of all 16th and 17th century English records in the IGI shows that most people named WINKLEY did reside in Co. Lancashire primarily along the River Ribble. There is a WINKLEY Hall at Aighton. The Winkleys were minor nobility there. They held two manor houses and were prominent professional men at Preston the county town for Lancashire. Numerous WINKLEY wills survive for this area as do numerous WINKLEY names in parish entries. Therefore it was not unreasonable for earlier genealogists to concentrate on Lancashire in their search for the birth of Samuel WINKLEY, but with a complete lack of success.

Research by the author in England, especially at the County Record Office at Preston turned up no baptism record for Samuel WINKLEY. In fact the name of Samuel was not found in any Lancashire records of the WINKLEY family.

In the book <u>Documents Relating to the WINKLEY Family</u>, by F.A. Winkley (1862) which is about the WINKLEY family in England, is found the following statement:

"There is a family of Winkleys in America who are descended from Samuel WINKLEY who left England about the year 1680. The family have a tradition that he went from Co. of Lancaster, where he left an older brother . . ."

The name of WINKLEY is also found in Co. Lincolnshire around the parish of Cowbit. Research by the author through records there failed to find the baptism of Samuel WINKLEY.

In Co. Devonshire there is a parish named Winkleigh. Research in that parish proved to be of no help. But in South Devon at long last success was achieved. In the parish of Dawlish the baptism of Samuel son of Nicholas WINKLEY on 1 Oct. 1660 was found. Further research into records for Co. Devon and with the assistance of Mr. Michael J.L. Wickes, [AGRA] a local Devon genealogist, the proof was established with a high degree of certainty. WINKLEY MANOR is found close to Dawlish on the border of the parishes of Woodbury and Colaton Raleigh. Its significance was not investigated.

The author presents the following pedigree based on the information he found.

WINKLEY FAMILY

Medieval records list a **ROGER de WYNKLEIGH** dean of Exeter Cathedral 1231 to 1262, when he died. [Burnet Morris Index Cards, Devon Record Office] In 1409 a **NICHOLAS WYNKELEY** and wife **JOHANNA** recorded at Brixham. [Devon & Cornwall Notes & Queries XIV/351] In the City of Exeter in 1343 is named a **JOHN de WYNKELEGH** a draper. He was fined £1. [1343 Mayors Court Rolls 16/17 Edw 3] In the 1524 Devon Lay Subsidy Roll at Galmeton (in Churston Ferrers parish) was a **THOMAS WYNKLEY** [T.L. Stoate, Devon Lay Subsidy rolls 1524-7, Bristol (1979)] See page 23 for complete list of Medieval Winkley names.

EARLY GENERATIONS

The name of WINKLEY first occurs at Dawlish in 1543. Both a Thomas and a William WINKLEY are named in the 1543 Devon Lay Subsidy Roll. We next find the same two names listed in the 1569 Devon Muster Roll and once again these same two names appear in the 1581 Devon Lay Subsidy Roll. While they could be the same two men it is more likely that they were father and sons, since a period of 35 years elapsed. The Thomas WINKLEY named in the 1581 Roll was probably the one born in 1569. Perhaps William was his brother.

In early Dawlish records are found two female WINKLEY names. A "Mother WINKLEY", midwife was paid 7 pence in 1597/8. She might be the mother of Thomas (2). In 1601/2 an Elizabeth WINKLEY is named in the Churchwardens accounts. She may be a sister of Thomas (2), if not a wife of William WINKLEY.

Unless additional information should be found in England, these earlier generations can not be resolved with any degree of certainty.

1. **THOMAS WINKLEY** Dawlish, Co. Devon.

He is named in the 1543 Devon Muster Roll at Dawlish. Perhaps a descendant of the **THOMAS WYNKLEY** named in the Devon lay Subsidy Roll 1524 at Churston Ferrers if not the same man. He was father or brother of **WILLIAM WYNKLEY** named in 1543 and 1569 Devon Lay Subsidy rolls.

Children: i. **WILLIAM**, 1569 & 1581 Lay Subsidy.
    2. ii. **THOMAS**,
      iii. **JOHAN**, md. 12 Apr. 1573 **JOHN CLIVE** at Stokeinteignhead. Had: **CHRISTOPHER**, bp 5 Nov. 1573, **PETER**, bp 2 Feb. 1576, **ELIZABETH**, bp 2 Dec. 1677, **ANNE** bur. 21 Jan. 1580 & **GILLIAN** bp 22 May 1582.

2. **THOMAS WINKLEY** Dawlish, Co. Devon.

He was born about 1559 probably at Dawlish. He was age 60 in 1619. He could have been the son of **THOMAS WYNCKLEY** named in the 1569 Muster Roll, or of **WILLIAM WYNCKLEGH**. Either he or his father was named in the 1581 Devon Lay Subsidy Roll. [£3 goods] He married **JOHANE CLARKE** about 1590. She is named in the Calendar of Devon Deeds. He is named as a sailor in 1619 at Dawlish. His age is given as 60 years. He is listed in the 1624 Devon Lay Subsidy Roll at Dawlish. He could have been the father of the following children if not their grandfather.

Children: i. **WELTYN**, d. 20 Mar. 1620, md. 3
               May 1606 **CLEMENT PREWE**, at
               Woodbury.
           ii. **JOANE**, md. 9 July 1627 **ROBERT**
               WISE. Had: **JEAN**, bp 14 July 1630.
    3.   iii. **WILLIAM**, md. 16 Oct. 1628 **MARRIAM**
               WAYNE.
    4.   iv. **NICHOLAS**, md. 19 Jan. 1632 **MARY**
               HEADON.

3. WILLIAM WINKLEY Dawlish, Co. Devon.

He was born about 1605 probably s/o **THOMAS** [2]
if not his grandson. He married 16 Oct. 1628
MARRIAM WAYNE. She buried 16 Aug. 1655 called
widow. He is named in the 1641 Protestation
Return. Possible children:

Children: i. **MARY**, md. 23 Sep. 1655 **GEORGE**
             VESY. Had: **ANDREW**, bp 14 Dec.
             1675.

4. NICHOLAS WINKLEY Dawlish, Co. Devon.

He was born perhaps in 1610 s/o **THOMAS** [2] if
not his grandson. He was buried 29 Mar. 1687 at
Dawlish. He married on 19 Jan. 1632 **MARY HEADON**.
She probably was the daughter of **RICHARD HEADON**
master mariner named in 1619 Devon Maritime
Survey. She might be the **AGNES** wife of **NICHOLAS**
buried 24 Oct. 1667. He married 2nd 9 Jan. 1668
MARY d/o **JOHN FRYER** at St. Thomas by Exeter
parish. He is called "Mariner of Dawlish." She
was buried 9 Nov. 1687, called widow. He is
named in the 1641 Protestation Record. He was
the Nicholas WINKLEY who witnessed the will of
Richard Seaward in 1662/3 at Portsmouth, NH.
This is proven by comparing his signature with
that on the 1668 Marriage License at Exeter.

1662 Signature
Portsmouth, NH

1668 Signature
Exeter, Devon, England

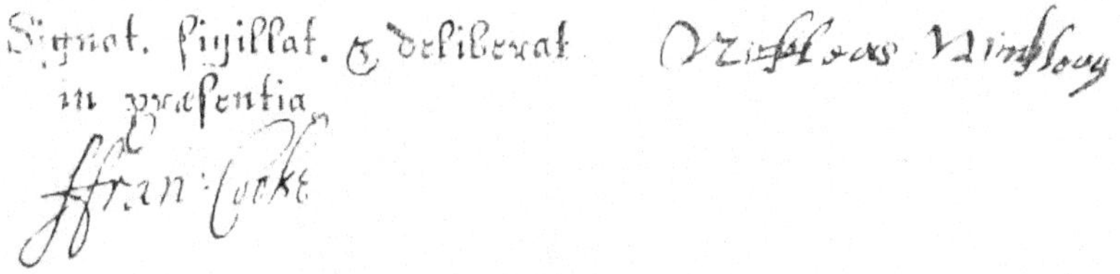

[handwritten signature in Latin script]

They probably had additional children but due
to the English Civil War the parish register is
incomplete. He was not named in the 1662 Hearth
Tax List because he was in New England. He is
listed in the Dawlish Overseer of the Poor
Accounts from 1670 to 1687.

Children: i. **JOANE**, d. 5 Feb. 1635.
            ii. **NICHOLAS**, twin bp 1 Jan. 1635/6,
               d. 23 May 1637.
          iii. **AVIS**, twin bp 1 Jan. 1635/6, d.
               5 May 1638.
          iv. **ELLENOR**, bp 18 June 1638.
gap to 1652;
           v. **MARY**, bp 1655 (betw 12 May & 18
               Aug.) md. 30 July 1667 **THOMAS**
               WIES.
   5.   vi. **WILLIAM**, b. c1657, d. c1694, md.
               31 Jan. 1680 **ELIZABETH FRIEND**.
   6.   vii. **SAMUEL**, bp 1 Oct. 1660, emigrated
               to Portsmouth, NH in 1680.
        viii. **THOMASIN**, had **NICHOLAS** bp 2 Sep.
               1671 (base born), md. 15 Oct.
               1671 **JOHN WILLS** at St. Thomas by
               Exeter by license. Both of
               Dawlish.

5. **WILLIAM WINKLEY**   Dawlish

He was born about 1657 at Dawlish the son of
NICHOLAS [4]. He died about 1693/4. He married
31 Jan. 1680 **ELIZABETH FRIEND** at Dawlish. She
was the daughter of **JOHN FRIEND**. She was bp. 23
Aug. 1663 at the adjacent parish of Mamhead. He
had the following children baptized at St.
Gregory, Dawlish. Was he the older brother who
remained in England? He is named in the Dawlish

church Wardens' Accounts from 1686 through 1693,
then his widow is named. He typically paid a tax
of 1 shilling.

An **ELIZABETH WINKLEY** possibly the widow of
WILLIAM, married 3 Dec. 1695 **RICHARD BOODEN.**
They had a daughter **ELIZABETH** bp 17 Mar. 1698.

Children: i. **MARY**, bp 1 Nov. 1681, d. Jan.
               1681/2.
          ii. **ELIZABETH**, bp 20 May 1683, d. 22
               July 1683.
         iii. **THOMASINE**, bp 2 July 1685, d. 8
               Jan. 1686.
          iv. **THOMASINE**, bp 21 Apr. 1687.
           v. **WILLIAM**, bp 19 June 1690.

6. **SAMUEL WINKLEY** Dawlish & Portsmouth, NH

He was baptized 1 Oct. 1660 at St. Gregory,
Dawlish the son of Nicholas 4. He most likely
emigrated to Portsmouth, NH on 9 Aug. 1680. He
became the founder of the WINKLEY's in New
England. See PART 2 for the WINKLEY line in New
England.

No burial before 1759 or marriage before 1700
or baptism of any children for Samuel WINKLEY
was found in the Dawlish P/R or other adjacent
Devon Parishes. Because of the rarity of the
name of WINKLEY we may assume that **SAMUEL
WINKLEY** was the immigrant. His name does appear
in later Devon records. He is named in the
Dawlish Overseer of the Poor Accounts and in the
Dawlish Churchwardens' Accounts after the death
of his father in 1687 up to 1711. No doubt he
inherited property at Dawlish.

HEADON FAMILY

1. MARY HEADON   Dawlish

She was born about 1615 possibly the daughter of
RICHARD HEADON [3]. She married 19 Jan. 1632
NICHOLAS WINKLEY at St. Gregory, Dawlish. [P/R]
She probably was the **AGNES** wife of **NICHOLAS
WINKLEY** buried 24 Oct. 1667 at Dawlish. See the
WINKLEY Section for her children.

2. RICHARD HEADON   Dawlish

Probably the son of **RICHARD HEADON [3]**. He had
the following children bapt. at St. Gregory,
Dawlish: [P/R]

Children: i. **EDWARD**, bp 19 July 1652.
           ii. **Son**, bp 16 Apr. 1655.
          iii. **JOHN**, bp 17 Dec. 1657.
           iv. **SARAH**, bp 30 Aug. 1660.

3. RICHARD HEADON/HAYDON   Dawlish

He was born c1574. He was a master mariner. He
was named in the 1619 Devon Maritime Survey and
in the 1641 Protestaion Return for Dawlish. He
was the father of the following children.

Children: 1. **MARY**, b. c1615, md. 19 Jan. 1632
              NICHOLAS WINKLEY.
           2. **RICHARD**,
          iii. **WYLMOTH**, (m), bp 8 Oct. 1609.
           iv. **JOHN**, named in 1641 Protestation
              Return at Dawlish.

CLARKE FAMILY

1. JOHANE CLARKE   Dawlish

She was born c1570. She married **THOMAS WINKLEY** (2) about 1590. She is named in the Calendar of Devon Deeds Enrolled At quarter Sessions for 26 Sep. 1616. She could have been the daughter of Henry Clarke named in the 1581 Devon Lay Subsidy roll. See WINKLEY section for her children.

2. HENRY CLARKE   Dawlish

He is named in the 1569 Devon Muster Roll and in the 1581 Devon Lay Subsidy Roll along with a JOHN CLARKE a possible son. He could be the son of **JOHN CLERKE** named in the 1524 Devon Lay Subsidy Roll at Dawlish.

Children: 1. **JOHANE**,
            ii. **JOHN**,

PEDIGREE CHART

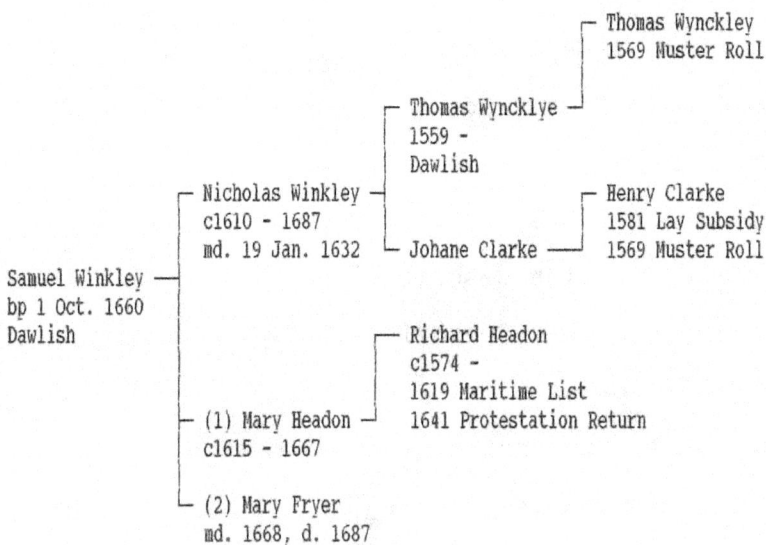

```
                                              ┌─ Thomas Wynckley
                                              │  1569 Muster Roll
                              ┌─ Thomas Wyncklye ─┘
                              │  1559 -
                              │  Dawlish
             ┌─ Nicholas Winkley ─┤              ┌─ Henry Clarke
             │  c1610 - 1687      │              │  1581 Lay Subsidy
             │  md. 19 Jan. 1632  └─ Johane Clarke ──┘  1569 Muster Roll
Samuel Winkley ─┤
bp 1 Oct. 1660  │
Dawlish         │              ┌─ Richard Headon
                │              │  c1574 -
                │              │  1619 Maritime List
                ├─ (1) Mary Headon ─┘  1641 Protestation Return
                │  c1615 - 1667
                │
                └─ (2) Mary Fryer
                   md. 1668, d. 1687
```

APPENDIX   PART 1

ST. GREGORY, DAWLISH, CO. DEVON

Parish Records:

```
1627 July 9  Joane Winckley - Robert Wise                        md.
1628 Oct. 16 William Winckley - Marriam Wayne                    md.
1630 July 14 Jean, d/o Robbert Wise                              bp.
1632 Dec. 19 Nicholas Winckley - Mary Headon                     md.
1635 Jan. 1  Nicholas & Avis, s. & d/o Nicholas Winckly          bp.
1636 Feb. 5  Joane Winckly                                       bur.
1637 May 23  Nicholas Winckley                                   bur.
1638 May 5   Avice Winckley                                      bur.
1638 June 18 Ellenor, d/o Nicholas Winckly                       bp.
1655 Sep. 23 Mary Winckley - George Vesy, sailor                 md.
1655 __ 20   Mary, d/o Nicholas Winkley                          bp.
1655 Aug. 16 Maria Winckly widow                                 bur.
1660 Oct. 1  Samuel, s/o Nicholas Winkley                        bp.
1667 July 30 Mary Winckley - Thomas Wies                         md.
1667 Oct. 24 Agnes, wife of Nicholas Winkly                      bur.
1671 Sep. 2  Nickolas, base born son of Thomazen Winkley         bp.
1675 Dec. 14 Andrew, s/o Gorge Vesy                              bp.
1680 Jan. 31 William Winckley - Elizabeth Friend                 md.
1681 Nov. 1  Mary, d/o William Winkley                           bp.
1681 Jan. _  Mary, d/o William Winckley                          bur.
1682 July 22 Elizabeth, d/o William Winkley                      bur.
1683 May 20  Mary, d/o William Winkley                           bp.
1685 July 2  Thomasine, d/o William Winkley                      bp.
1686 Jan. 8  Thomasin, d/o William Winckley                      bur.
1687 Mar. 29 Nicholas Winckley                                   bur.
1687 Apr. 21 Thomasine, d/o William Winckley                     bp.
1687 Nov. 9  Mary Winkley widow                                  bur.
1690 June 19 William, s/o William Winkley                        bp.
1695 Dec. 3  Elizabeth Winckley - Richard Booden                 md.
1698 Mar. 17 Elizabeth, d/o Richard Booden                       bp.
1732 Sep. 13 Mary Winckley                                       bur.
```

Source: Dawlish P/R and BT at Devon Record Office.
     Bapt. 1609, 1650 - 1750
     Md.   1627 - 1750
     Deaths 1627 - 1750

DAWLISH: OVERSEERS OF THE POOR ACCOUNTS:
1665-1713

1670 Nicholas Winckley gave 2 shillings.
1671 Nicholas Winckley gave 3 shillings and 6 pence.
1672 Nicholas Winckley gave 2 shillings and 6 pence.
1673 Widow Winckly gave 4 shillings.
1673 Nicholas Winckly gave 2 shillings and 6 pence.
1674 Nicholas Winckley gave 2 shillings and 11 pence.
1675 Nicholas Winckly gave 3 shillings and 4 pence.
1676 Nicholas Winckley gave 3 shillings and 4 pence.
1677 Nicholas Winckly gave 3 shillings and 9 pence.
1678 Nicklas Winckly gave 3 shillings and 4 pence.
1679 Nicolas Wincley gave 4 shillings and 7 pence.
1683 Nicholas Winckley gave 4 shillings and 4 pence.
1684 Nicholas Winckley gave 5 shillings.
1685 no record of Winkleys.
1686 Nicolas Winkly gave 5 shillings and 10 pence.
1687 Nicholas Winckly gave 5 shillings and 10 pence.
1688 Samuell Winkley gave ??
1689 Widow Winkley gave 4 shillings.
1690 Samuel winkeley or occupier gave 1 shilling.
1691 Samuell Winkley gave ??
1692 Sam Winkley gave 10 pence.
1693 Sam Winkly gave 10 pence.
1694 Samuel Winkley gave 2 shillings and 9 pence.
1694 William Winkley gave ??
1695 Samuell Wincaley gave 1 shilling and 2 pence.
1696 no record of Winkleys.
1697 Sam Winkley gave 2 shillings and 6 pence.
1698 Samuell Winckley gave 1 shilling and 1 pence.
1699 Samuell Winckley gave 1 shilling and 1 pence.
1700 Sam Winckley gave 1 shilling.
1701 Sammall Winkley gave 9 pence.
1702 no record of Winkleys.
1703 Sam Winckley gave 9 pence.
1704 no record of Winkleys.
1705 Sam Winkley gave 10 pence.
1706 no record of Winkleys.
1707 Sam Winkley gave 1 shilling.
1708 Samuel Winkley gave 1 shilling and 2 pence.
1709 missing pages.
1710 Samuel Winkley gave ??
1711 Sam Winkley gave ??

no record of Winkleys on later year rates.

DAWLISH: CHURCHWARDENS' ACCOUNTS: 1686-1712

1686 Nicolas Winkly gave 2 shillings and 1 pence.
1686 William Winkly gave 1 shilling.
1687 Nicholas Winckley gave 1 shilling and 3 pence.
1687 William Winckley gave 1 shilling.
1688 Nicholas Winkley gave 1 shilling and 3 pence.
1688 William Winkley gave 1 shilling.
1689 Nicholas Winckley gave 1 shilling and 3 pence.
1689 William Winckley gave 1 shilling.
1690 Nicholas Winckley gave 2 shillings and 6 pence.
1690 William Winckley gave 1 shilling.
1691 Samuel Winkley gave 4 pence.
1691 William Winkley gave 1 shilling.
1692 Sam Winkley gave 4 pence.
1693 William Winkley gave 1 shilling.
1694 Samuel Winkley gave 3 pence.
1694 Widow Winkley gave 6 pence.
1695 Samuell Winckley gave 4 pence.
1696 Samuell Winkley gave 0 pence.
1697 Samall Winkley gave 10 pence.
1698 Sam Winkley gave 4 pence.
1699 Samuell Winkley gave 3 pence.
1700 Samuel Winckly gave 3 pence.
1701 Sam Winckly gave 3 pence.
1702 Samuell Winkley gave 3 pence.
1703 Sam Winckley gave 3 pence.
1704 Sam Winkley gave 7 pence.
1705 Samuell Winkley gave 3 pence.
1706 Samuel Winkley gave 3 pence.
1707 Samuel Winkley gave 4 pence.
1708 Samuel Winkley gave 5 pence.
1709 Samuel Winkley gave 5 pence.

No Winkleys on later year rates.

Dawlish: Other Records:

Church Wardens' Accounts 1588 - 1606:

1597/8   Paid for Gregory Bond to Mother
          Wynckly who was left to paye: 7d.

1601/2   Paid the charge which was bestowed on
          the Ringers at Elizabeth Wyncklighes
          and William Mittens with candells the
          reivysinge (?) daie of our Queenes
          Majesty: 6s, 10d.

Calender of Devon Deeds Quarter Sessions:

1616 Sep. 25   Manor of Coffeton alias Coughton
          in Dawlish. . . . Richard Farrington
          holds there about 16 acres of land in
          the right of Elizabeth his wife by
          copie granunted . . . 14 Nov. 1577 for
          her life and after to Johane Clark,
          now wife of Thomas Winckley.

Devon Lay Subsidy & Muster Rolls:

1543-5	Thomas Wyncle	£2	goods
	William Wynkley	£1	goods
1569	Thomas Wynckley	£7	goods
	William Wyncklegh	£7	goods
1581	Thomas Winkely	£3	goods
	William Winkely	£5	goods
	Henry Clarke	£9	goods
	John Clarke	£3	goods
1624	Thomas Winkleye		

Devon Maritime Survey:

1619   Thomas Wynklye, sailor age 60 years
          Richard Haydon, master mariner 43 yrs
          John Clarke, sailor, age 21 years.

Devon Protestation Returns:

1641   Nicholas Winkley
          William Winckley
          Richard Headon

Hearth Tax Lists:

1662 and 1672   nothing found.

WINKLEY NAMES IN ADJACENT SOUTH DEVON PARISHES:

Ashcombe:

1695 July 11 Agnes Winkley - Elias Weekes md.

Brixham:

1543   Ebbett Wyncle £1 goods, Devon Lay Subsidy Roll.

Churston Ferrers:

1524   Thomas Wynkley £2 goods, Devon Lay Subsidy Roll.

Ermington:

1524   William Wynkeley £1 wages, Devon Lay Subsidy Roll.

Heavitree

1604 Jan. 16 Richard, s/o Richard Seaward   bpt.

Kingsbridge

1524   Sander Wybklegh £4 goods, Devon Lay subsidy Roll.

St. Thomas by Exeter:

1668 Jan. 9 Nicholas Winckley of Dawlish - Mary d/o John Fryer   md.
1671 Oct. 14 Tomasin Winckley - John Wills, both of Dawlish   md.

Stoke In Teignhead:

1573 Apr. 12 Johan Winklie - John Clive   md.
1573 Nov. 5   Christopher, s/o John Clive   bpt.
1576 Feb. 2   Peter, s/o John Clive   bpt.
1577 Dec. 2   Elizabeth, d/o John Clive   bpt.
1589 Jan. 21 Anne, d/o John Clive   bur.
1582 May 20   Gillian, d/o John Clive   bpt.

Woodbury:

1572 Apr. 7 Richard, s/o Henry Seawarde	bp.
1606 May 3 Weltyn Winkley (f) - Clement Prewe	md.
1620 Mar. 13 Weltsine Prewe	bur.
1676 Oct. 16 Henry, s/o Henry Branfill	bp.
1682 Oct. 4 Thomas, s/o Henry Branfill	bp.

Adjacent parishes search. No Winkley names
found:

    Bishopsteignton   Sheldon St. Nicholas

    Combeinteignhead   Withcombe Raleigh

    Mamhead

MAP OF DAWLISH, COUNTY DEVON

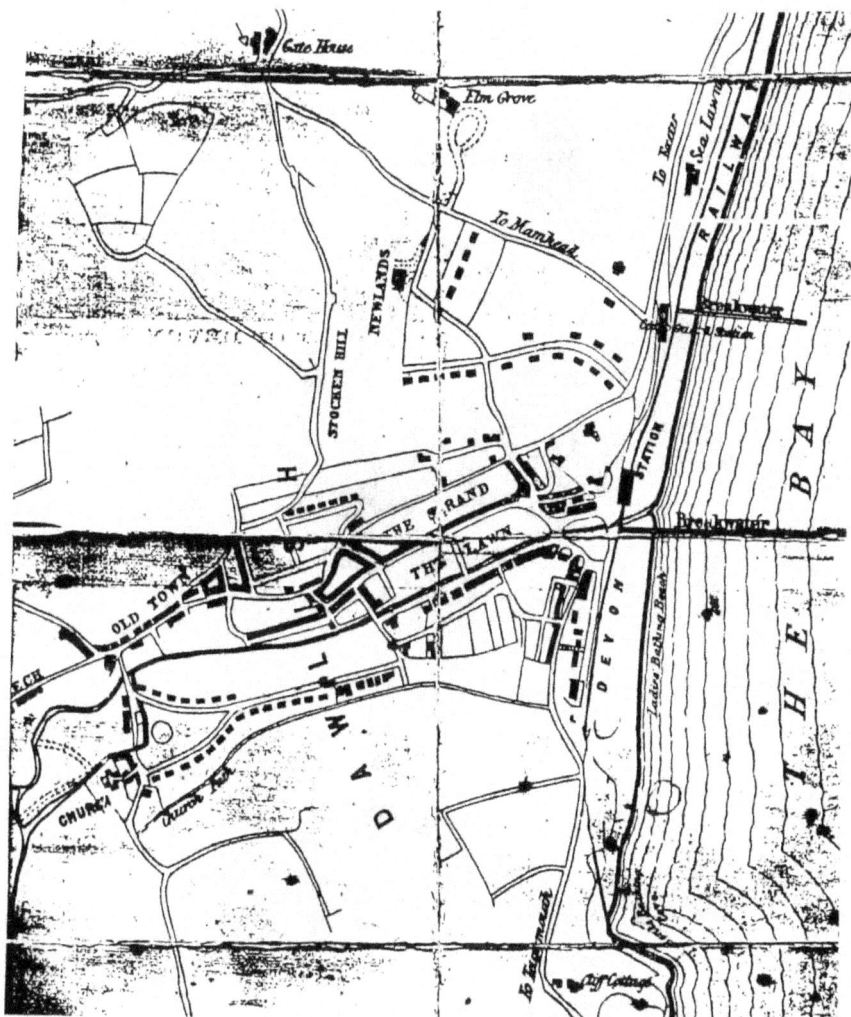

Source: Dawlish Walks, Drives & Excursions,
        W,M, Cornelius, Dawlish (c1880)

From a drawing by]   DAWLISH PARISH CHURCH.   *[Gordon Home.*

DAWLISH PARISH CHURCH

The parish church today is called St. Michael, but was called St. Gregory in the 17th century. When or why the alternation took place can not now be traced.

Of the original thirteenth - century building, only the tower remains. The rest was rebuilt in 1825. The interior was again wholly renewed in 1897. A brass tablet on the west wall commemorating this last restoration.

No old monuments in the church are obviously antiquity save two seventeenth - century tombs near the south door.

Source: Dawlish, The Estuary of the Exe, B.T. Cresswell (1902). [At Westcountry Library, Exeter, England]

PORT OF DAWLISH

Dawlish was one of six ports at the mouth of the
River Exe in South Devon, England. See Map on
page 2. The others in 1619 were Kenton,
Powderham, Exmouth, Lympston and Topsham. [Devon
& Cornwall Rec. Soc., New Series, v.33] In 1619
at Dawlish there were named 15 Masters/Mariners,
103 sailors and 15 Seinemen. Under the list of
ships at Dawlish was one named "Mayeflower" of
12 tons. It is not thought to have been the one
that took the Pilgrims to New England in 1620.

In 1619 there were listed some 53 ships at the
Exe Estuary or 22% of all South Devon ships. Of
these ships over 1/3 were fishing vessels at
Newfoundland. This shows a strong connection
with North America at an early date. The ships
varied in size from 10 up to 120 tons.

There was one ship named PROPEROUSE, but it is
doubtful that it was the ship of the same name
owned by Richard Seward of Portsmouth, NH some
43 years later. The later Prosperous might have
been captained by Nicholas WINKLEY.

Records of Dawlish as a port are found as early
as 1301. It had a lighthouse in 1881 [The
Maritime Hist. of Devon, M.M. Oppenheim, Exeter
(1968)] Regretfully Port Books of ship arrivals
and departures have not survived.

WINKLEY MANOR

Winkley Manor was located in the parish of
Colaton Raleigh. See map on page 2. It is listed
on the Index of Manorial Court Records at Devon
Record Office, Exeter, England as early as 1635
etc. [Mormon film #1526651] Today what remains
is called Winkley Farm.

MEDIEVAL DEVON WINKLEY RECORDS

1219 JOHN de WINKELEY, rector of Portlemouth in Devon, and his brother REGINALD.

1228 ROGER de WYNLEIGH, served as archdeacon of Totnes (1228-1231), dean of Exeter Cathedral (1231-1252). He died in 1252.

1273 MICHAEL de WYNKELEY, recorded as a juror at Budleigh.

1274 RICHARD de WYNKELEGH, recorded as a juror at Winkleigh.

1293 MICHAREL de WINKELEGH, recorded in manor survey at Stockleigh Pomeray.

1295 MICHAEL de WINKELEGH recorded as a witness at Woodbury.

1300 NICHOLAS de WYNKELEGH recorded as tenant of tenement in Exeter belonging to Robert Richemond. Also mentioned "the tenement which formerly belonged to MICHAEL DE WYNKELEGH and ADAM DE WYNKELEGH.

1316 JOHN de WYNKELEGH tenement in Exeter listed.

1332 RICHARD WYNKELEGH taxed 12d at Lympstone.
      RICHARD de WYNKELEGH taxed 12d at Clyst St. George.
      JOHN de WYNKELGH taxed 2s 6d at Crediton.

1343 JOHN de WYNKELEGH draper at Exeter fined £1.

1362 RICHARD WYNKELEYE & others accused of robbing from shipwrecks at Plymouth.

1369 THOMAS de WINKLEGH parson of Thedbridge in Devon.

1401 GEOFFREY WYNKELEY, chaplain in Exeter diocese involved in maritime legal dispute.

1409 NICHOLAS WYNKELEY and his wife JOHANNA recorded at Brixham.

1455 WILLIAM WYNKELEY appointed controller of the search in ports of Exeter and Dartmouth.

1507 THOMAS WYNKLEY and his wife involved in brawl at Dartmouth with Thomas Whyte, as recorded in proceedings of Mayors court.

1524 SANDOR WYNKLEGH in Devon Lay Subsidy Roll at Kings bridge.
      THOMAS WYNKLEY in Devon Subsidy Roll at Galmenton (Churston Ferrars)
      WILLIAM WYNKLELEY in Devon Lay Subsidy Roll at Ermyngton.

1569 WILLIAM WENCKLY recorded as warden of the weavers company in Exeter.

SOURCES:

1. Burnet Morris Card Index Devon Record
   office, Exeter, England. Read by Mr. Wickes.

2. Exeter Freeman 1266-1967, Margary M. Rose,
   Exeter (1977)

3. Index to Devon Record Office deeds before
   1840. Read by Mr. Wickes.

4. Devon Lay Subsidy 1524-7, T.L. Stoate,
   Bristol (1979)

5. Exeter Mayors Court Rolls 16/17 Edw 3.

6. Devon & Cornwall Record Society, n.s. V. 14
   (1969)

WINKLEY - LANCASHIRE

The name of WINKLEY is quite ancient in the area around Preston, Co. Lancashire, England. William WINKLEY Jr. in his book *Documents Relating to the WINKLEY Family*, Harrow Press (1863) presents pedigree charts that trace the family name back to the 12th century. An Alexander is the first so named. Regretfully the proof provided for these pedigree charts seems to be lacking and needs further documentation. There is little doubt that the WINKLEY name has existed in the Ribble River Valley for hundreds of years. They were nobility.

WINCKLEY HALL was an estate in Aighton township of the parish of Mitton. Winckley Hall is now a ruin. It stood on the right bank of the River Hodder, where it enters the River Ribble. In the 17th century Robert de Wynckedlegh resided there.

The WINKLEY name was very prominent in the records of Preston, the county town for Lancashire. Preston was a major seaport there before the ships got to big to enter the river. The Winkleys were wealthy business men at Preston. Numerous Gild Rolls named Winkleys at Preston. [The Record Soc. Lanc. & Cheshire, Preston Guild Rolls, 1397, 1682, v.9 (1882)] Weaving was an important industry at that time. Thomas WINCKLEY was the mayor four times around 1700. WINCKLEY Square, an area of four acres, in the city center is named for him. WINCKLEY Club which opened in 1846 having 100 members is located on the east side of the square. [Hist. of Preston, England, A. Hewitson (1883)] About the same time the Winkleys owned Banistre Hall in the adjacent parish of Walton-le-Dale.

The author has researched extensively the parish records, old will and the like for the Ribble River Valley area of Co. Lancashire at the County Record office. No record of the birth of anyone named SAMUEL WINKLEY was found.

Surprisingly the name of Samuel wasn't used by the Winkleys. Many persons named WINKLEY were found. One problem in looking for the baptism is that it occurred at the time of the English Civil War. Cromwell and all that trouble. Churches were used as stables by Cromwell's soldiers. Parish registers were not kept up or were lost.

In the mid 1600 there were two large areas of Winkleys in the Ribble River Valley. One group lived at Mitton and Richester (an old Roman town). The other group resided in Preston and Walton-le-Dale. The Winkleys held Baristre Hall at Walton-le-Dale.

Tradition says that Samuel WINKLEY came from Co. Lancashire. Some earlier researchers even state he was born at the city of Clitheroe. The author has visited the town of Clitheroe, site of the famous English witch trials. No record of Samuel's birth nor record of anyone name WINKLEY was found in the parish register. The probable reason for naming Clitheroe as his birth place is the fact that it is the closest major town to the site of WINCKLEY Hall, the ancient home of the WINCKLEY nobility.

The earliest record found by the author of a WINKLEY was in 1367 Richard de Wynkeleye attorney for Nicholas de Haryngton. Named in Lancashire Knights of the Shire, v.96, New Series.

While no one named Samuel WINKLEY was found the name of Nicholas WINKLEY occurred frequently. A list of findings follows:

1406 Jan. 28 Nicholas de Winkley, Chaplain of Ashton.
1550   Nicholas, s/o Anthony Winkley named at Dutton.
1560 Oct. 3   Roger Winkley will at Woodfield names Nicholas Winkley as a witness.
1566   Anthony Winkley will at Altham names son Nicholas.
1574 Apr. 28 Katherine Winkley w/o Anthony will at Mitton names her son Nicholas. Nicholas married a dau. of Holden of Chaigley.
c1600   Nicholas s/o William Winkedeley at Banastre Hall [34E1]

1622 May 2   Elsabeth d/o Nycholas Wynckeley buried at Blackhurst.
1625 July 4   Nycolas Winkley of Dutton buried at Ribchester.
1625 Feb. 20 Hary s/o Nycholas Winkeley bpt. at Blackhurst.
1629   Harry s/o Nycholas Winkeley bpt. at Blackhurst.
1675 Feb. 25 Henry s/o Nicholas Winckley of Haighton buried at Broughton-
              near-Preston.
1677 June 23 A child of Nicholas Winckley buried at Broughton-near-Preston.

None of these Nicholas Winkleys found would appear to have been the Nicholas WINKLEY who witnessed the 1662/3 will of Richard Seward of Portsmouth, NH. They can all be ruled out.

William Winkley Jr. reported his findings of Winkley names in Co. Lancashire and even some in Cambridgeshire, Middlesex and Norfolk. How he failed to discover Winkley Manor and the Winkley names in Devonshire is a mystery. If he had done so the origin of Samuel Winkley would have been uncovered years earlier.

                                        W.H.J.

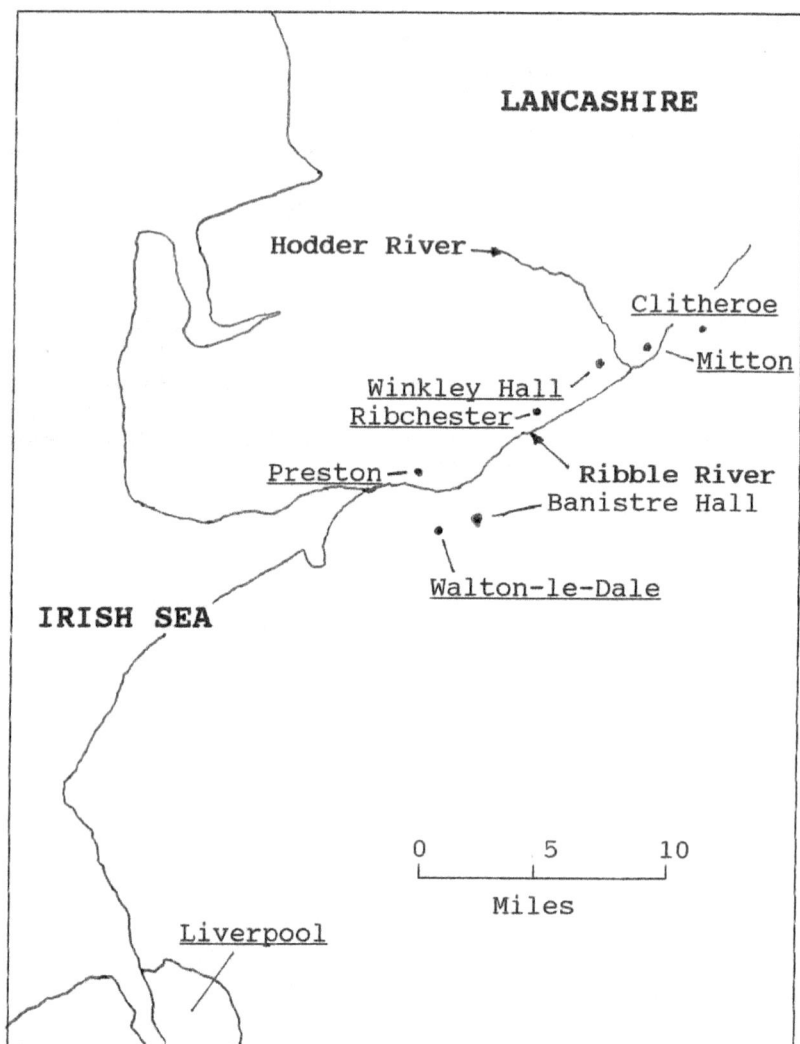

LANCASHIRE

Hodder River →

Clitheroe

Mitton

Winkley Hall
Ribchester

Ribble River
Banistre Hall

Preston

Walton-le-Dale

IRISH SEA

0   5   10

Miles

Liverpool

WINKLEY - LINCOLNSHIRE

The name of WINKLEY is found in the southeast corner of County Lincolnshire, England. The name appears about the middle of the 16th century. There is a tradition that the WINKLEY's are descended from one of the Lancashire house, which during some civil or religious upheaval took refuge here. The earliest record found was the will of William Winkley at the parish of Irby dated 28 Feb. 1542. He names his sons Thomas, John and Robert and daughter Jelian, all under age. [Documents Relating to the WINKLEY Family, Wm Winkley Jr, Harrow, p. 15, 1863]

The WINKLEY's resided mainly at the parish of Cowbit, but bapt and marriages are found in many adjacent parishes in the 1600's. No record of any one named SAMUEL was found. The name of NICHOLAS occurs at Cowbit starting in 1610. There were at least three so named. Uncle and nephews? None appear to have been mariners nor emigrated to New England. Briefly what was found was:

1. **NICHOLAS WINKLEY** - s/o JOHN of Pechhall in parish of Holland. Named in fathers will May 1610. John requested to be buried in chapel yard of Cowbite. Nicholas had brothers RICHARD (b. 1605) and THOMAS (b. 1607) and sisters HELLEN and JANE.

2. **NICHOLAS WINKLEY** - s/o HENRY. He was bapt. 1 June 1615 at Cowbit and died by 1622. Henry WINKLEY md. 6 Oct. 1614 ALICE TURLTEBIE at Cowbit. Henry witnessed the 1610 will of John. Brothers? Henry had 5 additional children bapt at Cowbit. Namely: JOHN 1617, ALICE 1619, ISABELL 1623, JOAN 1625 and ANN 1628. [Cowbit P/R]

3. **NICHOLAS WINKLEY** - s/o HENRY. He was bapt. 1 Sep. 1622 at Cowbit. He married 11 June 1640 ALICE HARRISON at Spaulding. Had a daughter ONNER bp 1645 at Cowbit. His will dated 30 Jan.

LINCOLNSHIRE Cont.;

1653 at Pickdall. [PCC, 304 Brent] He names wife
ALICE, son ROBERT and daughter ANN. A ROBERT
WINKLEY witnessed his will. [Spaulding & Cowbit
P/R's]

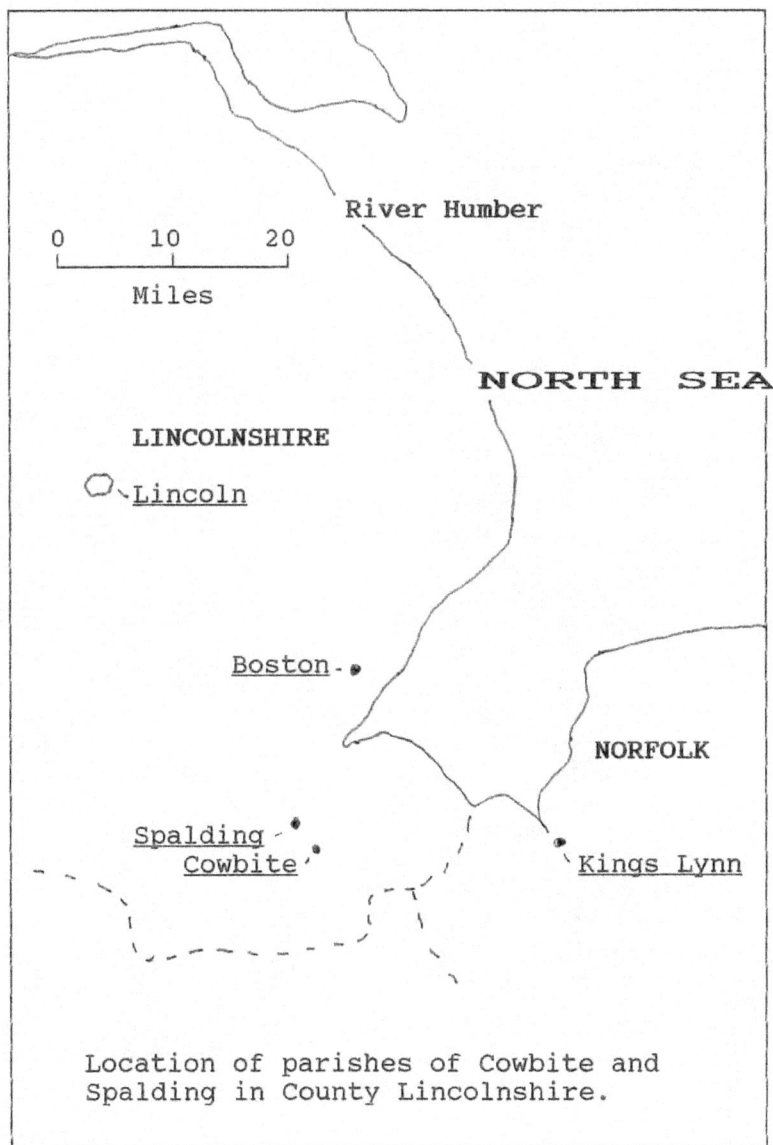

River Humber

0   10   20
Miles

NORTH SEA

LINCOLNSHIRE

Lincoln

Boston

NORFOLK

Spalding
Cowbite

Kings Lynn

Location of parishes of Cowbite and
Spalding in County Lincolnshire.

1668 Marriage License of Nicholas Winkley & Mary Fryer at St. George by Exeter, Devon.

Noverint universi per praesentes nos Nicholaum Winkley de Dawlish in Com. Devon nautam, et Samuelem Calle Civ. Civit. Exon Goldsmyth — teneri & firmiter Obligari Reverendo in Christo Patri & Domino Domino Antonio — providentia divina EXON: Episcopo in Centum — libris bonae & legalis monetae Angliae Solvend. eidem Reverendo patri aut suo certo in hac parte Attornato, Executorib. Administratoribus, Successoribus vel Assignatis suis. Ad quam quidem solutionem bene & fideliter faciend. Obligamus nos & utrumque — nostrum per se pro toto & in solido, Haeredes, Executores & Administratores nostros firmiter per praesentes Sigillis nostris sigillat. dat. nono — die Januarii Anno Regni Dom. nostri Caroli Secundi Dei gratia Angliae Scotiae Franciae & Hiberniae Regis Fidei Defensoris &c. vicesimo — — —
Annoque Domini 1668

The Condition of this Obligation is such, That if hereafter there shall not appear any lawfull Let or Impediment by reason of any precontract, Affinity, Consanguinity, or any other lawfull means whatsoever, but that the above bounden Nicholas Winkley and Mary Fryer daughter of John Fryer of St. Thomas [illegible] in Devon, [illegible] — may lawfully solemnize Matrimony, and in the same afterwards remain and continue like Man and Wife according to the Laws of this Realm in that behalf provided; And if there be not at this present any Action, Suit, Plaint, or other Demand had or moved for or concerning any such lawfull Let or Impediment. And if the said Parties do not proceed to the solemnization of the said Marriage without the consent of their Parents or Governours; And if the said Marriage be openly solemnized in the Church between the hours of Eight and Twelve in the Fore-noon, according to the Book of Common-Prayer by Law established. And lastly do defend and save harmless the said Reverend Father and all his Officers and Ministers whatsoever against all Persons whatsoever, for or concerning the granting of a Licence in this behalf. Then this Obligation to be void and of none effect; Or else to stand remain, and be in full power, force, and vertue.

Signat. sigillat. & deliberat in praesentia
Fran: Cooke

Nicholas Winkley

Samuel Calle
Exon

PART 2

WINKLEY FAMILY IN NEW ENGLAND

1680 - 1900

NEW HAMPSHIRE & MAINE

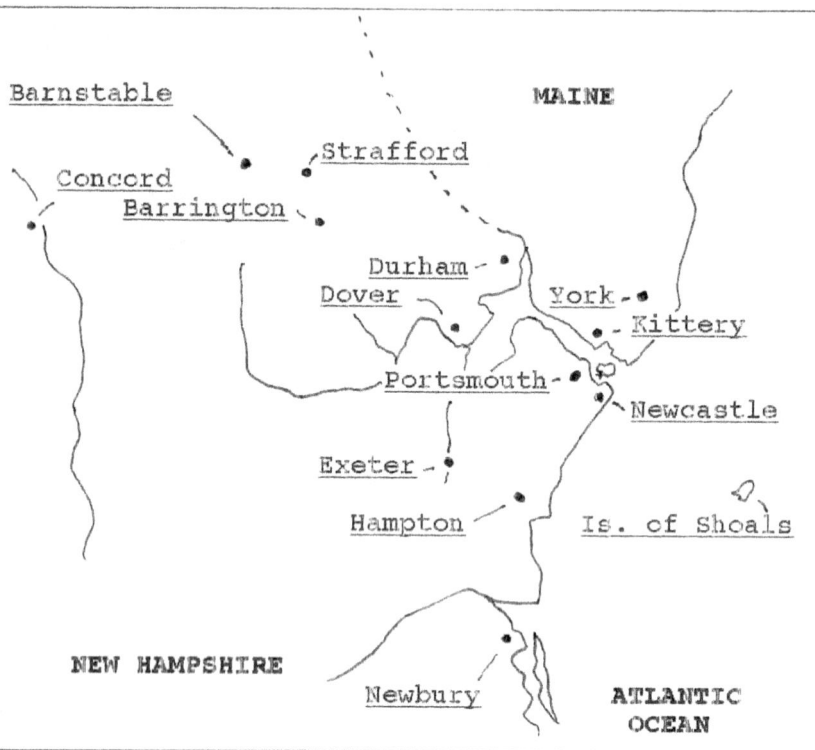

Barnstable

MAINE

Strafford

Concord

Barrington

Durham

Dover

York

Kittery

Portsmouth

Newcastle

Exeter

Hampton

Is. of Shoals

NEW HAMPSHIRE

Newbury

ATLANTIC
OCEAN

The descendants of Capt. Samuel WINKLEY have
been researched by a number of genealogists.
Articles in journals and manuscripts can be
found at such libraries as NHHS, Concord, NH and
NEHGS, Boston, MA. The earliest article known
was published in the *Dover Enquirer*, 1 May 1862
entitled *HISTORICAL MEMORANDA No. 221 WINKLEY
FAMILY*. [Copy at NH State Library] No researcher
has presented any English origin proof for
Samuel Winkley. See page 104.

The Author compiled the following descendants
of Capt. Samuel Winkley to aid persons tracing
this family. Information was taken from the
sources named in the Bibliography on page 108.
The information should be verified before full
acceptance. Only the authors own Winkley line
has been verified.

1. **SAMUEL WINKLEY** Boston, Kittery and Portsmouth

He was baptized 1 Oct. 1660 at St. Gregory,
Dawlish, Co. Devon, England the son of **NICHOLAS
WINKLEY**. [Dawlish P/R] He died in 1736 at
Portsmouth, NH. His will is dated 13 Nov. 1726
and was proved 6 May 1736 [see Appendix for
complete will] He was married three times. He
married first at Kittery, Me. in 1684 **SARAH**, d/o
FRANCIS TRICKEY. (some source give his name as
THOMAS TRICKEY) [Stearns, NH Gen. p. 1132] She
died by 14 May 1705 at Boston, Mass. He married
second, 12 Dec. 1705 in Boston **HANNAH (CHECKLEY)
ADAMS**, d/o **ANTHONY CHECKLEY** and widow of **JOHN
ADAMS**. She died by Feb. 1707/8, probably at
Boston. He married third in Portsmouth, NH North
Church in Nov. 1712 **ELIZABETH (HUNKING) FERNALD**,
d/o **JOHN & ANN (HUNKING) HUNKING** of Isles of
Shoals. [NHGR 5:41] She died 6 Aug. 1723 and is
buried at Point of Graves cemetery in Portsmouth
[NH Gen. Rec. 1:19] His occupation was mariner,
ship builder, Captain and merchant. He resided
at Portsmouth, Kittery and Boston. In Kittery he
lived on Crooked Lane. Afterwards moved to
Portsmouth, NH.

Samuel was the master of the ketch **MARY** of Kittery in 1683, which brought tobacco into New Hampshire. Master of the ketch **ADVENTURE** in 1686. Bound to Jamaica in 1691. Samuel Winkley is named in a 1692/3 petition for a separate township for New Castle. [Gen. Dict. of Me. & NH] He was paid 10s in the 1693 Treasurer Statement by the Providence of NH [NH Prov. Papers 17:621-2] On 25 May 1694 Samuel Winkley of Newcastle was paid £2..5 for powder money Imported, under the disbursements in 1694/5. [NH Prov. Papers 17:644-8, 32:288-291]

Nathaniel Fryer, President of Council wrote 12 June 1694 "Mrs Winkley, you are required in their magisties name to lodge William Powel, Jacob Smith and Jonathan Norris." [NH Prov. Papers 17:635-9] Sarah Winkley's account for the above lodging was allowed in Council on 10 Jan. 1694/5:

"To dressing 3 men, 9 days at 6 pence,
        7 shillings.
To 9 nights lodging at 6 pence night,
        7 shillings, 6 pence.
To 4 meals for 3 men at 4 pence meal,
        4 shillings."

Samuel witnessed the Will of Ann Jeofrey of Kittery on 9 July 1695 [York Deeds 4:155] In July 1696 Samuel is 5th name on list taken oath of allegiance to the crown, at New Castle. [Gen. Dict. Me. & NH] He is named on tax lists 1698 - 1700 at Great Island. [Gen. Dict. Me. & NH] Samuel had a complaint at the General Assembly of the Council at Portsmouth, 9 July 1700, in regard to liquor taxes paid. [NH Prov. Papers 3:105] He imported and exported rum and molasses. On 10 May 1703 the Town of Kittery granted Samuel 100 acres of land. [York Deeds, 22 Feb. 1712/3] He moved to Crooked Lane in Kittery about 1703. Occupied 20 acres that had been owned by his wife's father Francis Trickey. [Me. Prov. & Court Rec. v4, p.158] [Old Kittery & Her Families, Everett Stakepole (1903]

The 20 acre grant made in 1656 to Francis Trickey, fisherman, reached from Crooked Lane to Spruce Creek. It was laid out to Samuel Winkley in 16 May 1702. The annual value in 1712 was £4.

Because of difficulties with the French in Nova Scotia in 1707 three regiments of about 500 men each were raised for the conquest of Port Royal. They were defeated. Samuel owned a sloop **SARAH & HANNAH** which was impressed for service as a troop transport. Abraham Lewis of Greenland was impressed as the pilot. Samuel was the commander 17 April 1707. [NH Prov. Papers 2:502-8]

Evidence was found in Dawlish, Co. Devon records that he inherited some property there. He began paying taxes after the death of his father in 1687. His name last appears in 1711. He obviously was an absentee landlord. Perhaps he sailed to Dawlish on occasion, but this is only speculation. [Dawlish Overseer of the Poor Accts. & Dawlish Churchwardens' Accts.]

He was a land owner in Kittery, Me. in 1712 [Stackpole, Hist of Kittery, p. 149-151] Taxed to So. Church in Portsmouth in 1717 [Gen. Dict. Me. & NH] In 1719 he bought the Hoddy House in Portsmouth from Capt. Paul & Mary (Hoddy) Gerrish. [Gen. Dict. of Me. & NH] Taxed in Grafford Lane in Portsmouth in 1722. In 1722 Samuel is on the list of Portsmouth business men granted propriety rights in the new Town of Barrington. He was granted 200 acres. [Hist. of Barr., p.17-8] Justice of Peace, 29 Apr. 1730 [Rock. Rec. Lib 17, p. 150]

Samuel Winkley's Will was dated 13 Nov. 1726. He made bequests to his sons Francis, Nicholas, William and Samuel. Names his daughters Elizabeth Weeks, Sarah Langdon and kinswoman Elizabeth Hunking. His old servant Mary Grant was left a silver spoon. His bequests included much real estate, silver and other household goods. His will was proved 6 May 1736 [NH Prov. Papers 32:288] The final division of the estate took place on 26 Feb. 1745/6 [NH Prov. Papers 32:288-294] Son Francis got the house and land in Crook Lane, Kittery, Me. See APPENDIX for complete copy of his will. Children according to Old Kittery & Her Families:

Children: 2. **SAMUEL**, b. 28 Oct. 1687, d. 18 May 1708 at sea, unmd.
3. **FRANCIS**, b. c1689, d. 23 Apr. 1776, md. 12 Nov. 1724 **MARY EMERSON**.
4. **SARAH**, md. 12 Feb. 1713/4 **TOBIAS LANGDON**.
5. **NICHOLAS**, b. c1694, d. 1 June 1739, md. **SARAH WADE**.
6. **MICHAEL**, b. 13 May 1699, d. 18 May 1699 at Kittery.
7. **WILLIAM**, b. 5 Feb. 1700, md. **SUSANNA CUTTS PENHOLLOW**.
8. **JOHN**, d. 18 Oct. 1703 at Boston.
9. **ELIZABETH**, b. c1703, d. 23 Feb. 1748, m.1, **SAMUEL WEEKS**, m.2 13 Oct. 1741 **JOHN WHEELWRIGHT Jr.**
by 3rd wife:
10. **SAMUEL**, bp 12 Nov 1721, d. by 1737, md. **OLIVE PHIPPS**. [NHGR 5:38]

SECOND GENERATION

2. **SAMUEL WINKLEY** [SAMUEL 1] He was born 28 Oct. 1686/7 probably at Great Island (New Castle). He never married. He died at sea 18 May 1708. He was master of the sloop **SARAH & HANNAH**, his fathers ship. Sailed back and forth to Virginia in 1707.

3. **FRANCIS WINKLEY** [SAMUEL 1] He was born about 1689 probably at Great Island, NH or Kittery, Me. and died 23 Apr. 1776 possibly at Barrington, ae 87 years. He married 12 Sep. or Nov. 1724 at Portsmouth, NH [NEHGR 24:18] **MARY EMERSON, d/o Rev. JOHN & MARY (BATTER) EMERSON** by Hon. Joshua Pierce. She was born about 1704 and died 17 Mar. 1745, age 41.

He was a ship captain and boat builder. He
learned his trade in Boston [Amer. Ancestry
5:60] He witnessed the will of Timothy Wentworth
10 May 1705 [York Deed v.5, Bk vii, fo.
38] and witnessed will of Peter Lewis 2 June 1713 [York
Deed v.8, Bk viii, fo. 179] His sister Sarah
Langdon and husband quit claimed the Kittery
estate to Francis 2 Nov. 1727 [York Deed v.12,
Bk xii, fo. 189] No doubt he took over the
Crooked Lane property when his parents went to
Boston about 1703. His wife was admitted to the
So. Church in Portsmouth 14 Mar. 1731 [NEHGR
81:437] after 1745 they moved to Barrington, NH
where he built his house on Smoke Street. Was
J.P. Children born in Kittery. [NH Geneal.
Digest, Glenn Towle, 1986]

Children: 11. **JOHN**, b. 9 Feb. 1725/6, bp 13
Feb, d. 31 Mar. 1811, m.1
DOROTHY FURBISH, m.2, 18 Jan.
1758 **DEBORAH KEEN/CAIN**. [NEHGR
24:357 & 81:437]
12. **ELIZABETH**, b. 7 Nov. 1728, bp 10
Nov., d. 23 Nov. 1806, unmd. Liv.
Barrington [NEHGR 81:437]
13. **SAMUEL**, b. 9 Mar. 1730/1, bp 14
Mar., d. 29 Nov. 1806, md. **MARY
BREWSTER**. [NEHGR 81:437]
14. **FRANCIS**, b. 25 Oct. 1733, bp. 28
Oct., d. 9 Oct. 1818, md. 1763
MARTHA HUNKING. [NEHGR 81:437]
15. **MARY**, b. 21 June 1737, d. 1 Dec.
1776, unmd at Boston, Mass.
16. **EMERSON**, b. 4 June 1740, bp 29
June, d. 17 Sep. 1810, unmd.
Liv. Barrington, NH.
17. **SARAH**, b. 1741, d. 6 Feb. 1803,
md. 21 May 1759 **NATHANIEL STEVENS**
at Boston.

4. **SARAH WINKLEY [SAMUEL 1]** She was born c1695.
She married 12 Feb. 1713/4 at Portsmouth's North
Church **TOBIAS LANGDON**, s/o **Capt. TOBIAS & MARY
(HUBBARD) LANGDON**. He was born 11 Oct. 1789 at
Rye, NH. [Brewsters Rambles around Portsmouth].
[NEHGR 23:269] Children named LANGDON:

Children: i. **MARY**, b. 4 Oct. 1717.
          ii. **TOBIAS**, b. 22 Dec. 1719.
         iii. **SARAH**, b. 2 Mar. 1721/2.

5. **NICHOLAS WINKLEY** [**SAMUEL 1**] He was born 1694
or 1702 probably at Great Island, NH, and died 1
June 1739 at Portsmouth, NH. He signed marriage
intentions 27 Apr. 1724 with **Mrs. MARY NOWEL** of
York, Me. but didn't marry her. He married about
1729/1730 **SARAH WADE**, d/o **Rev. JOHN & ELIZABETH
(GERRISH) WADE**. Occ. captain and mariner. Res.
Boston, Mass. 1726. His will admin. granted 25
July 1739 to widow SARAH. Inventory attested 26
Sep. 1739 £304.5.7. by John Ayers & John
Shackford. [NH State Papers 32:759]

Children: 18. **SARAH**, d.s.p. 1758.
          19. **ELIZABETH**, md. **WILLIAM HILL**, of
              Portsmouth, NH.

7. **WILLIAM WINKLEY** [**SAMUEL 1**] He was born 5
Feb. 1700. Alive 1770. He married **SUSANNA CUTTS
PENHOLLOW**, d/o **SAMUEL & MARY (CUTTS) PENHOLLOW**.
She born 10 Jan. 1708 and died 8 Aug. 1781.
[NEHGR 32:31] Occ. boat builder and mariner.
Res. Boston 24 Oct. 1728 and Portsmouth, NH. He
wit. will of Henry Seward, shipwright of
Portsmouth, proved 13 Apr. 1737. He wit. will of
Shackford proved 11 Mar. 1730/1. He wit. bond of
Mary Prisco widow of Exeter 21 Jan. 1732/3.
SAMUEL PENHALLOW came from St. Mabon Co.
Cornwall, England. [Farmer, First Settlers of
N.E.]

Children: 20. **WILLIAM**, b. 15 Apr. 1739, md. 1
              Jan. 1766 **ELIZABETH LEE**.

9. **ELIZABETH WINKLEY** [**SAMUEL 1**] She was born
about 1703 at Boston and died 23 Feb. 1748 age
43. She married first by March 1724/5 **SAMUEL
WEEKS** of Boston. She married second 13 Oct. 1741
JOHN WHEELWRIGHT Jr. of Wells, Me. Had a son by
second husband.

10. **SAMUEL WINKLEY** [SAMUEL 1] He was born after 1708 and was bapt. 12 Nov. 1721 at No. Church in Portsmouth [NHGR] and died by 1737. He married **OLIVE PHIPPS**, d/o **THOMAS & MARY (PLAISTED) PHIPPS**. According to Probate Records he was insolvent. [NH State Papers 32:635] She married second after 16 Apr. 1740 **CYPRIEN JEFFREY**.

THIRD GENERATION

11. JOHN WINKLEY [FRANCIS 3] He was born 9 Feb.
1725/6 probably at Kittery, Me., bp 13 Feb. and
died 31 Mar. 1811, age 85 years at Kittery. He
married first 2 Sep. 1749 **DOROTHY FURBISH** and
married second 18 Jan. 1758 **DEBORAH KEEN**, d/o
JOSEPH KEEN/CAIN. She born 1734 and died 27
Mar. 1829 age 95 years. [NEHGR 81:437] Enlisted
in Rev. War 1775, Capt. Wm Deering Co. of
carpenters. Res. Kittery, Me. [Kittery and her
Families, p. 802-3]

John inherited the crooked Lane place and was a
carpenter, boat builder and mariner like his
father and Uncles. Named in 1790 census at
Kittery, Me. [2-0-5]. pp 61.

Children: 30. JOSEPH, d.y.
           31. FRANCIS, b. c1765, d. at sea,
               md. 26 Sep. 1791 **MARTHA BROWN**.
           32. JOHN Jr, b. 20 Feb. 1767, d. 18
               May 1813, md. **LYDIA HOIT**.
           33. ELIZABETH/LYDIA, md. 18 Aug.
               1787 **WILLIAM BOOTHBY** of
               Limerick, Me.
           34. MARY/POLLY, md. 15 Nov. 1789
               JOHN STONE of Limerick, Maine.
               [NEHGR 63:175]
           35. SARAH, md. 8 July 1795 **WILLIAM
               TIBBETTS** at Wakefield, or
               Brookfield, NH.
           36. DORCUS, b. 10 Aug. 1782, md.
               _____ **WIGGEN** of Brookfield.
           37. ESTHER, md. **JOSEPH BENSON**, of
               Kittery.
           38. DOROTHY, md. Dec. 1799 **JOSEPH
               BLANY** in Ports. [Notice from NH
               Gazette, Otis Hammond, 1970]
           39. MARTHA, md. _____ **COTTON**, of
               Portsmouth.

13. SAMUEL WINKLEY [FRANCIS 3] He was born 9
Mar. 1730/1, probably at Kittery, Me. and bapt.
14 March following at South Church Portsmouth.
[NEHGR 81:437] He died 29 Nov. 1806 at
Barrington. He married **MARY BREWSTER**, d/o **SAMUEL**

& MARGARET (WATERHOUSE) BREWSTER. She born 13
Apr. 1734 and died 3 Nov. 1816, age 82.
[Brewster, Rambles Around Ports. v.2, p. 99]
Occ. carpenter & joiner. Served his time with
Mark Langdon of Ports. [1862 Dover Enquirer]
Went to Barrington about 1750. He signed the
Association Test at Barrington on 3 Sep. 1776
[NH Prov. Papers p.302] Shaker Elder. Public
Service Rev. War. Res. Barrington, N.H. His will
dated 10 Aug. 1803 and proved 7 Dec. 1807. Named
wife Mary & sons Samuel, Francis, William, John,
Benjamin & David. Named daughters Mehitable
Tasker, Elizabeth Layn & Mary Edgerly. [Staff.
Co. Prob. 10:528] Purchased Lot #92 & 93 in 1764
for £1500 from John Whidden, joiner of Ports.
[NEHGR 125:95] Deed 27 Oct. 1763 land in
Barrington #427. Named in 1790 census at
Barrington, NH [2-1-3].

Children: 41. **SAMUEL Jr.**, b. 24 Dec. 1756, bp
               16 Jan. 1757, d. 18 May 1812,
               md. **OLIVE KINGMAN**.
           42. **FRANCIS**, b. 28 Mar. 1759, d. 20
               June 1847, m.1, 16 Sep. 1781
               SARAH L. LIBBY, m.2, **DORIS** _____
               _____.
           43. **MEHITABLE**, b. 10 May 1761, d. 22
               Sep. 1824, md. **PAUL (JOHN)**
               TASKER s/o **JOHN & MARY (YOUNG)**
               TASKER of Barnstead. No ch.
           44. **WILLIAM**, b. 31 Aug. 1763, d. 29
               July 1845, m.1, 20 Nov. 1785
               MARTHA CLARK, m.2, **MARY WINKLEY**
               [#53], m.3, **TAMSON PIERCE**.
           45. **JOHN**, b. 17 Nov. 1766, d. 8 Jan.
               1843, md. 14 Nov. 1791 **MARY**
               SWAIN.
           46. **ELIZABETH**, b. 9 Mar. 1769, d. 29
               July 1850, md. **EDMOND LAYN**.
           47. **BENJAMIN**, b. 3 Jan. 1772, d. 30
               Sep. 1851, md. **ELIZABETH PITMAN**.
           48. **DAVID**, b. 4 July 1775, d. 18
               Dec. 1852, md. 4 July 1802 **ANNA**
               HUSSEY.
           49. **MARY**, b. 3 Aug. 1777, md. 28
               Dec. 1797 **ELIAS EDGERLEY**.

14. **FRANCIS WINKLEY [FRANCIS 3]** He was born 25 Oct. 1733 at Kittery, Me. and bapt. 28 Oct. 1733 at South Church Portsmouth, N.H. He died 29 Nov. 1806 or 9 Oct. 1818 at Barrington, N.H. [NHGR p. 1132] He married by 1763 **MARTHA HUNKING**, d/o **Capt. MARK & MARY (LEAVITT) HUNKING.** She born 1734 at Portsmouth and died 10 Jan. 1807 age 73 at Barrington, N.H. He was a selectman. Signed the Assoc. Test 3 Sep. 1776 at Barrington. [NH Prov. Papers v30] Res. Barrington. His will dated 21 Sep. 1818, proved Nov. 1818. [Staff. Co. 22:202] Named in 1790 census [3-0-3] and 1800 census [11011/01101]

Children: 50. **MARK HUNKING**, b. 28 Oct. 1763,
                 d. 28 Oct. 1843, md. **TAMSON
                 HAYES**.
            51. **MARY**, b. 15 Feb. 1766, d. 6 Oct.
                 1835, md. **WILLIAM WINKLEY**. [#44]
            52. **JOHN**, b. 8 Oct. 1769, d. 8 Apr.
                 1859, md. 12 Feb. 1801 **RUTH FOYE**
            53. **MARTHA**, b. 16 May 1771, d. 18
                 June 1859, md. 20 Jan. 1803
                 SHEDRECK DREW.
            54. **FRANCIS**, b. 1774, d. 6 Apr.
                 1855, md. 28 Feb. 1799 **SARAH
                 DREW**. (if not his cousin #41)
            55. **SARAH**, b. 1776, d. unmd. 28 Aug.
                 1845, at Barrington. [65-5-20]

16 **EMERSON WINKLEY [FRANCIS 3]** He was born 4 June 1740 and bapt. 29 June following. He died 17 Sep. 1810. His wifes name is unknown. Listed in 1790 [1-0-2] and 1800 census, York Co., Me. [11001-10011] Served in Kittery militia in Rev. War.

Children: 56. **daughter,**

20. **WILLIAM WINKLEY [WILLIAM 6]** He was born 15 April 1739 at Portsmouth, N.H. He married 1 Jan. 1766 **ELIZABETH LEE** at the South Church. [NEHGR 82:292] She died 8 Aug. 1781. Occ. boat builder. [NEHGR 81:302] Res. Portsmouth, N.H.

Children: 60. **WILLIAM KNIGHT**, b. 20 July 1766

FOURTH GENERATION

31. FRANCIS WINKLEY Esqr. [JOHN 11] He was born 1765 at Kittery, Me. and died 16 Apr. 1799 at sea [Notices from the NH Gazette, Otis Hammond 1970]. He married 26 Sep. 1791 **MARTHA BROWN** d/o **THOMAS & DOROTHY (DEERING) BROWN** of Kittery. She b. c1770. Called Captain. Res. Portsmouth, N.H.

Children: 70. **MARTHA ANN MARY**, b. 1804 at
                Kittery, md. 21 Mar. 1824 **SETH**
                LEIGHTON at Dover. Had: **JOHN**,
                CHARLES WILLIAM, **JANE ANN** md.
                CHAS. E. MAIN. [NH Gaz. 3:94]
            71. **JOHN Jr.**, b. 5 May 1793, [AF] d.
                1826, md. **JANE STEVENS HOBART**.
            72. **WILLIAM**,

32. JOHN WINKLEY Jr. [JOHN 11] He was born 20 Feb. 1767 at Kittery and died 18 May 1813 age 46. He married 24 Apr. 1799 **LYDIA HOIT/HIGHT** at Newington, NH. She died with Shakers at Canterbury, NH. [NHGR 1:151] Occ. clockmaker. Res. Durham, N.H. [Gen. Records of Durham, NH. v1, p. 151] Named in 1790 census at Barrington [1-0-0]

Children: 73. **JAMES FOLSOM**, b. 4 July 1802, d.
                13 Sep. 1846 at Portsmouth, N.H.
                ?. md. **MARTHA HICKS**.
            74. **MARY ANNE FOLSOM**, b. 29 Sep.
                1804, d. 29 Aug. 1810 d.s.p. at
                Durham.
            75. **CHARLOTTE C.**, b. 11 Sep. 1807 or
                1811, d. at Shaker Village,
                Canterbury, md. **VALENTINE SMITH**.
            76. **CLARISSA**, d. at Shaker Village,
                Canterbury, NH.

41. SAMUEL WINKLEY Jr. [SAMUEL 13] He was born 24 Dec. 1756 at Barrington, NH, bapt. 16 Jan. 1757. [NEHGR 82:145] He died 18 May 1812 age 55. He married **OLIVE KINGMAN**. She born 1751 and died 17 Oct. 1822 age 71. [NHGR 3:46] Res. Rochester, Barrington and Lebanon, NH. Both buried in Nathaniel Caverly Cem. in Strafford, NH. His

will dated 21 Mar. 1812, proved 21 Aug. 1812
[Stafford 13:122]. Rev. War service, Enlisted 8
Sep. 1777. Fought at Bennington, Vt. In 1790
census at Barrington [1-1-4]

Children: 81. **ELIZABETH**, b. 16 Feb. and bp. 12
Aug. 1783, md. 8 Oct. 1806 **JONA.
DREW** of Durham.
82. **MARY**, bp. 12 Aug. 1783, md. 19
Jan. 1812 **RICHARD FURBER Jr.** of
Farmington.
83. **MEHITABLE**, b. 5 Aug. 1789, md.
12 Oct. 1811 **PIERCE P. FURBER**
of Farmington. Children.
84. **OLIVE,** bp 27 July 1806, unmd.
Will 5 May 1862.
85. **SAMUEL**, d.y. 9 July 1822 [28y.]
86. **ABIAH**, bp 27 July 1806, d. 24
Feb. 1881, md. 24 May 1824
AUGUSTUS ROLLINS, Esqr. s/o
**Capt. HIRAM & JOANNA (WENTWORTH)
ROLLINS** of Somerset/Rollinsford.
He b. 29 Aug. 1797, d. 27 Jan.
1870. [NHGR 6:34, 4:330] Had 5
ch. including **SAMUEL WINKLEY
ROLLINS**.

42. **FRANCIS WINKLEY [SAMUEL 13]** He was born 28
Mar. 1759 at Barrington, NH and died 20 June
1847 at Canterbury, NH. He married first 16 Sep.
1781 **SARAH L. LIBBY** at Dover, N.H. She d. May
1843, ae 84-10-27, a Shaker at Canterbury, NH.
He joined Shakers and became an elder. [NEHGR
25:58] Sons left Shakers and settled at
Amesbury, Mass.

Children: 87. **SAMUEL**, d.s.p., md. no issue.
88. **ENOCH**, b. c1782, md. 3 Mar. 1812
MARY LOCKE at Seabrook, NH.
89. **SWAIN**, md. **HANNAH HAMOND**.

44. **WILLIAM WINKLEY [SAMUEL 13]** He was born 31
Aug. 1763 at Barrington, N.H. [NHVR] and died
there 29 July 1845 age 82 yrs. [NH Bible Rec.,
314] He married first 20 Nov. 1785 **MARTHA CLARK**.
[Barrington T.R. 1:725] She b. 25 Feb. 1763 at

Barrington, NH, [ibid] d. 11 Oct. 1786, ae 23
yr. [NHVR]   He married second 27 Dec. 1787 **MARY
WINKLEY [#53]** his 1st. cousin. She born 15 Feb.
1766 [NHVR] died 6 Oct. 1836 [69-7]. He married
third Jan. 1836 **TAMSON PIERCE**, d/o **DEACON
BENJAMIN PIERCE** in Dover, NH. [NHVR] She b. 6
June 1780, d. 28 Jan. 1858. Did he marry fourth
SARAH HARVEY?? J.P. at Barrington for over 40
years. His will dated 17 Aug. 1840, proved 5
Aug. 1845 [61:190] Wife TAMMY got "all the
household furniture she brought with her." Sons
William & Samuel got all his farming utensils
and wearing apparel. Son Hunking got $10. The
four daughters received furniture after wifes
death. Buried Sunnyside Cem. in Barrington, NH.
Res. Barrington. 1790 census at Barrington [1-2-
1].

Children: 90. **PAUL T.**, b. 5 Oct. 1786, d. 28
                 Nov. 1830, md. 7 May 1809
                 ABIGAIL K. ROLLINS at Loudon.
by 2nd wife:
            91. **WILLIAM M. Jr.**, b. 13 Jan. 1789,
                 d. 23 May. 1866, md. 26 Nov.
                 1818 **SARAH HUSSEY**.
            92. **MARTHA M.**, b. 3 Jan. 1791, d. 11
                 Nov. 1818, age 28. [Quint. 308,
                 NH Bible Rec. 314].
by 3rd wife:
            93. **MARY**, b. 27 July 1793, d. 1 Sep.
                 1876, [Barr. Cem.] md. 18 Mar.
                 1818 **JOSEPH HUSSEY**. [NH Bible
                 Rec. 314] He d. 23 Dec. 1853 age
                 65 yrs. No children.
            94. **ANN**, b. 27 Jan. 1796, d. 11 Dec.
                 1871, md. 9 July 1822 **JEREMIAH
                 BUGGELL**. [Strafford Co. Md., 55]
                 6 children.
            95. **SARAH**, b. 22 Feb. 1798, d. 7
                 Dec. 1871 unmd. [NHVR]
            96. **HUNKING"HENRY"**, b. 9 Nov. 1803,
                 by 1862 unmd. Merchant NYC. unmd
            97. **SAMUEL**, b. 5 Oct. 1805, d. 17
                 Apr. 1863, m.1, 28 Dec. 1828
                 NANCY FOSS, m.2, 12 Mar. 1839
                 LYDIA FOYE.

> 98. **JOANNA**, b. 13 Dec. 1810, d. 8
> June 1887 at Rochester, md. 7
> June 1829 **WILLIAM HAYES**, 7 ch.
> [NH Family Rec. 311,312]

45. Dea. JOHN WINKLEY [SAMUEL 13] He was born 17
Nov. 1766 at Barrington, NH and died 8 Jan. 1843
age 77. He married 17 Nov. 1791 **MARY SWAIN**, d/o
RICHARD SWAIN of Barrington, N.H. She died 4
Feb. 1854, ae 90 yrs. Deacon of Church. His will
2 Sep. 1839, proved 7 Feb. 1843 [59:50] Son
Daniel executor. Had 99 ac. farm. Res.
Barrington and Stafford. Both buried Stafford
Corner Cem. Had 9 children of whom 6 grew to be
adults. 1790 census at Lancaster [1-0-2] [NH
Gen. Digest p.272]

Children: 100. **DANIEL**, b. 26 May 1792, d. 4
Feb. 1883, md. 20 Mar. 1816
SARAH OTIS.
101. **JOHN**, b. 1 Feb. 1795/7, d. 19
Oct. 1868, md. 9 Nov. 1815
SUSAN OTIS.
102. **SAMUEL**, md. **NANCY FIFIELD**, moved
to Plainfield, NH.
103. **SWAIN**, Boston, b. 11 Jan. 1802,
md. **HARRIET HAMMOND**.
104. **DAVID**, md. **MARIA LEWIS**, will 18
Dec. 1848, proved 4 Jan. 1855.
105. **MARY A./MARYAN**, m.1, 17 Sep.
1835 **Capt. DAVID K. MONTGOMERY**,
m.2, **STEPHEN P. BLAKE**. Moved to
W. Roxbury, Mass. Had: **JOHN S.**,
b. 18 May 1850 and **DAVID M.**
[Gen. Rec. Straff. Co. v18, #5,
1993]

46. ELIZABETH WINKLEY [SAMUEL 13] She was born
9 Mar. 1769 at Barrington, N.H. and died 29 July
1850. She married about 1800 **EDMOND LAYN** of Lee,
N.H. Children named LAYN.

Children: i. **SAMUEL LAYN**, b. 2 Aug. 1801.
ii. **MARY LAYN**, b. 29 Oct. 1802, md.
c1820 **TRUEWORTHY HILL**.
iii. **JOHN LAYN**, b. 26 Apr. 1804.

iv. **SUSAN LAYN**, b. 30 Dec. 1805
v. **EDMUND LAYN**, b. 7 Oct. 1807.
vi. **DAVID LAYN**, b. 9 Sep. 1809.

47. **BENJAMIN M. WINKLEY** [SAMUEL 13] He was born 3 Jan. 1772 at Barrington, N.H. and died 30 Sep. 1851 at Barnstead, N.H. He married first 7 Apr. 1795 at Barrington **ELIZABETH PITMAN**, d/o **SAMUEL & SARAH (SMALL) PITMAN** of Barnstead, by Rev. Wm Benj. Palde [NHVS]. She born 1775 and died 1841 age 66. He m.2, 17 Oct. 1841 **BETSEY CATE** at 80- Barnstead, NH. She b. 1778 and d. 28 Apr. 1863, 3-10 [NHVS]. Buried in Winkley Cem. in Barnstead. Occ. blacksmith. In 1806 owned part of Pitman saw mill. Res. Barnstead. Named in 1830 census.

Children: 106. **SARAH**, b. 22 Aug. 1795, d. 20 May 1884, md. **JAMES LEIGHTON**. Had: **VARNUM H.**
107. **SAMUEL**, b. 25 Nov. 1797/8, d. 24 Oct. 1872, md. 17 Jan. 1827 **MARY MARTIN**.
108. **BENJAMIN Jr.**, b. 1 Feb. 1800, md. 23 Nov. 1826 **ELIZA C. HOIT**.
109. **MEHITABLE**, b. 24 June 1802, md. 24 Nov. 1824 Capt. **JOHN FELKER**. 10 children. Res. Barrington.
110. **EBENEZER P.**, b. 12 Oct. 1804, d. 14 Mar. 1870, md. 14 Sep. 1836 **ELIZA WHITCOMB**.
111. **FRANCIS**, b. 2 Mar. 1807, d. 1849, md. 1832 **OLIVE HANNIFORD**.
112. **HANNAH P.**, b. 10 Aug. 1811/3, md. 13 Dec. 1832 **TRUE MASON**.
113. **WILLIAM PLUMMER**, b. 26 May 1816, d. 26 Jan. 1899, m.1, 25 Sep. 1842 **HELEN M. SIMONS**, m.2, 1 Jan. 1852 **MARY A. DOLBEER**.
114. **ELIZABETH ANN**, b. 30 June 1819, md. 18 July 1841 **JOHN B. TUTTLE** at Barnstead.
115. **DAVID B.**, b. 18 Sep. 1821 at Barnstead, NH, d. 9 Feb. 1908, md. 23 Jan. 1848 **MARY S. WEEKS**.

48. **Col. DAVID WINKLEY [SAMUEL 13]** He was born
4 July 1775 and died 18 Dec. 1852. He married 4
July 1802 at Barrington, NH **ANNA HUSSEY** d/o
RICHARD HUSSEY. She b. 1784, died 7 Nov. 1848 ae
64y. No children. Both buried Pine Grove Cem.
Barrington, N.H.   Perhaps the David WINKLEY
whose store burned 1812 at Concord, N.H. 1830
census at Barrington. [Hist. of Concord, NH,
Bouton] In 1850 Census living with Stephen P.
Blake at Barrington,

49. **MARY WINKLEY [SAMUEL 13]** She was born 3 Aug.
1777 in Barrington, N.H. She married 28 Dec.
1797 **ELIAS/SILAS EDGERLY** of Madbury, N.H. Res.
Barnstead. Children named EDGERLEY:

Children: i. **DAVID**,
            ii. **LOWELL**, b. 1811.
           iii. **SAMUEL**, b. 1813.
            iv. **LAURA**,
             v. **MARY**,
            vi. **MEHITABLE**,

50. **MARK HUNKING WINKLEY [FRANCIS 14]** He was
born 28 Oct. 1763 in Barrington, N.H. and died
28 Oct. 1842 at Strafford, N.H. He married 25
Aug. or Feb. 1791 **TAMSON HAYES**, d/o **PAUL HAYES
Jr.**, Esqr. of Alton, N.H. Occ. farming. Res.
Strafford. Single in 1790 census. 1800 census
[1011-2021] His will 23 Sep. 1837, proved 1 Nov.
1842 [Stafford 59:53]. 1830 & 1840 census at
Strafford.

Children: 120. **MARY/MERCY**, b. 27 Jan. 1792,
                 md. prob. by 4 June 1815 **Capt.
                 ISAAC Y. FOLSOM** of Alton.
            121. **FRANCIS**, b. 22 Mar. 1797, d. 18
                 Nov. 1862, md. 18 Apr. 1822
                 SARAH/SALLY N. LOUGEE.
            122. **MARTHA**, b. 1800, d. 1863, md.
                 c1819 **JOHN PERKINS Esq.** 4 ch.
            123. **PAUL**, b. 3 Feb. 1803, d. 15
                 Aug. 1870, md. 29 Nov. 1820/1
                 LYDIA M. JONES.
            124. **DENNIS**, b. 1808, d. 20 Jan.
                 1889, ae 79-7-24, md. 7 Apr.
                 1831 **MARY ANN HOWARD**.

51. MARY WINKLEY [FRANCIS 14] She born 15 Feb.
1766 and died 6 Oct. 1835. She married 27 Dec.
1787 her cousin **WILLIAM WINKLEY [#44]** as his
second wife. See #44 above for their children.

52. JOHN WINKLEY [FRANCIS 14] He was born
probably at Barrington, NH 8 Oct. 1769 and died
8 April 1859. [90-5-0] He married 12 Feb. 1801
RUTH FOYE d/o **STEPHEN & DEBORA (SWAIN) FOYE.** She
born c1780 and died 3 Feb. 1864 [84-5-0] Buried
family cem. opposite WINKLEY pond. Occ. farmer.
Res. Barrington, N.H. In 1850 Census.

Children: 130. **Capt. ASA,** b. 19 Dec. 1801, d.
27 June 1854, md. 29 Jan. 1828
HANNAH WINGATE.
131. **MARTHA,** b. 6 Mar. 1803, md. 12
Dec. 1826 **Col. WILLIAM STEARNS**
of Deerfield, Res. at
Portsmouth.
132. **JOHN HUNKING Jr.,** b. 14 Aug.
1805 or 1806, d. 27 May 1878,
m.1, 2 Mar. 1835 **KEZIAH BROCK,**
m.2, 1 Apr. 1851 **SUSAN
YOUNG BROCK.**
133. **JEREMIAH,** b. 8 July 1807, d. 16
July 1891, md. 2 Oct. 1831 **MARY
/MARIA JANE LANGLEY.**
134. **WILLIAM P.,** md. **PAMELIA CRANE.**

53. MARTHA WINKLEY [FRANCIS 14] She was born 16
May 1771 and died 18 June 1859. She married 20
Jan. 1803 **SHADRACK DREW.** Children named Drew:
[Hist. of Durham]

Children: i. **NICHOLAS V.,** b. 2 Jan. 1804, md.
ELIZA CHESLEY.
ii. **JEREMIAH,** b. 8 Nov. 1805, md.
CLARRISA NUTE of Dover.
iii. **SHADRACK,** b. 27 Oct. 1807 twin,
md. **SARAH BACHELDER** of Exeter.
iv. **MARTHA,** b. 27 Oct. 1807 twin, d.
21 Mar. 1810.
v. **LUCINDA,** b. 17 Nov. 1812, e. 17
Dec. 1831, md. **GEORGE HUEL/HURD?**
of Rochester.

vi. SARAH A., b. 14 Mar. 1815, d. 31
    Dec. 1831 unmd.

54. FRANCIS M. WINKLEY [FRANCIS 14] He was born
1774 at Barrington, NH and died there 6 April
1855. He married 28 Feb. 1799 SARAH/SALLY d/o
Capt. JOHN & TAMSON (DREW) DREW of Alton. She
died 26 March 1846, [68-6-0]. Her will 27 June
1843, proved 2 Sep. 1845 [61:193]. He married
2nd ABIGAIL CHURCH d/o NATHANIEL & MARY
(LEIGHTON) CHURCH. She born 22 Oct. 1796.
Occupation farmer. Probate #1832. In 1850 census
at Barrington.

Children: 135. JOHN HUNKING, b. 8 Feb. 1800,
                 md. 21 Mar. 1841 ELIZA CHOATE.
            136. GEORGE W., b. 16 Mar. 1802, md.
                 19 Feb. 1832 TAMSON STANTON.
                 Moved to NY State.
            137. TAMSON D., b. 4 Aug. 1804.
            138. DARUIS, b. 17 June 1807, m.1,
                 URSULA HILL/HALL, m.2, MARIA
                 DANIELS, m.3, SARAH CATE.
            139. CYRUS, b. 30 Nov. 1809, unmd.
                 Went to Wisc.
            140. MARTHA M., b. 8 May 1812, md.
                 B.F. WHIPPLE.
            141. JOSEPH, b. June 1814, d. 30
                 Oct. 1890, md. 11 Apr. 1840/1
                 MARY CATER.
            142. ABIGAIL H., b. 22 Jan. 1817,
                 unmd. to Wisc.
            143. FRANCIS M., b. 9 June 1821, md.
                 23 Mar. 1859 SARAH A. d/o
                 DANIEL & NANCY (CORNELL) BERRY.
                 She b. 8 Sep. 1839 at Ports.,
                 d. 12 Mar. 1924.

65. JOSEPH WENDECKER WINKLEY [unknown] He was
born 1775 in NJ and died 27 Mar. 1833 at
Holman's Ridge, Indiana. He married 19 Oct. 1806
MARY LYON. She born 1780 in NJ and died 1857 in
Dearborn County, Indiana. His will proved 14 May
1833. Son William and Thos. Baggs Admin.
[Dearborn Co. Probate Record Book, Chris.
McHenry 1986, p. 209] Moved to Dearborn County
in 1813. Settled on Holman's Ridge south of

Aurora. Bought land Sec. 5 in 1813. [Hist. of
Dearborn & Ohio Co., F.E. Weakley & Co., Chicago
1885, p. 426, 951] In 1830 census in Dearborn
County, Indiana. Probably not JOSEPH #30. [AF]

Children: 150. **WILLIAM**, b. 1807 Ohio, md. **SUSAN
KNICKERBOCKER**.
151. **JOSEPH WENDECKER Jr.**, b. 1812
Ohio, d. 5 Apr. 1857, md. c1931
ELIZABETH _____.
152. **MARY ANN**, b. 6 Apr. 1815 in
Ind., md. 26 Sep. 1833 **MARTIN
s/o WILLIAM & ELIZABETH (HESTER)
TRESTER**. He b. 27 May 1806 in KY
Had: **EMMA A**; **OLIVER H.**; **LEWIS
M.**; **ALBERT E.**; **MILTON L.**; **MARY
J.**; **JAMES H.** and **ELLA F.**
153. **JOHN L.**, b. 1816 in Ind.
154? **FRANCIS L.**, b. 1825, In 1850
census in White Co., Ind.

FIFTH GENERATION

71. JOHN WINKLEY [FRANCIS 31] He was born 1789
or 1793 and died 28 Sep. 1826 on the ship ELIZA
while at Hampton, Va. He married **JANE STEVENS
HOBART** d/o **Col. SAMUEL HOBART**. Called Captain.
He commanded 14 gun privateer FOX during the War
of 1812. [Amer. Anc. v.5:60] Res. Portsmouth,
N.H.

Children: 159. JOHN F., b. 17 Mar. 1817, md. 3
                  Feb. 1850 CAROLINE LEFAVOUR.
             160. SAMUEL HOBART, b. 5 Apr. 1819,
                  d. 1 Aug. 1911, md. 13 Aug.
                  1849 MARTHA W. PARKER at
                  Boston, Mass.

73. JAMES FOLSOM WINKLEY [JOHN Jr. 32] He was
born 4 July 1802 and died 13 Sep. 1846. Found
dead in woods at North Hampton NH [NEHGR 73:200]
He married **MARTHA HICKS**. Res. at Portsmouth, NH.
1840 census at Portsmouth. No children.

81. ELIZABETH WINKLEY [SAMUEL 41] She born 16
Feb. and bp. 12 Aug. 1783. She married 8 Oct.
1806 **JONATHAN DREW** of Durham, NH. Children named
Drew:

Children: i. SAMUEL W., b. 16 Jan. 1808.
           ii. JOSEPH, b. 12 Aug. 1811.
          iii. LUCINDA J., b. 29 Nov. 1812.
           iv. HORATIO, b. 3 Dec. 1814.
            v. AURELIA JANETTE, b. 27 May 1817.
           vi. JONATHAN R., b. 14 Apr. 1821.

83. MEHITABLE WINKLEY [SAMUEL 41] She born 5
Aug. 1789 at Farmington. She married 12 Oct.
1811 **PIERCE POWERS FURBER Jr.** Children named
Furber.

Children: i. MARY WINGATE, b. 11 Sep. 1812.
           ii. JOSEPH WARREN, b. 29 Aug. 1814.
          iii. THEODORE, b. 15 Mar. 1817.

88. **ENOCH WINKLEY** [FRANCIS 42] He born c1782. He
married 7 Feb. or 3 Mar. 1812 **MARY LOCKE** at
Seabrook, NH. She born c1792. Left Shakers and
settled at Amesbury, Mass. Named in 1830 census
and 1850 census at Amesbury, Mass.

Children: 175. **JOHN FRANCIS**, b. 20 Jan. 1815.
    176. **MARY S.**, b. 15 Oct. 1816, md.
      23 Dec. 1840 **WILLIAM CLEVELAND**
      BARTON at Boston.
    177. **SARAH L.**, b. 27 Mar. 1818, md.
      8 Nov. 1845 **AMOS R. BINNEY**.
    178. **FRANCIS JOHN**, b. 17 June 1830.

89. **SWAIN WINKLEY** [FRANCIS 42] He was born 11
Jan. 1802. He married **HANNAH HAMOND**.

Children: 180. **MARY**,
    181. **MARTHA**,
    182. **DAVID**,

90. **PAUL T. WINKLEY** [WILLIAM 44] He was born 5
Oct. 1786 at Barrington, NH and died 28 Nov.
1820. He married 7 May 1809 at Loudon, NH
ABIGAIL K. ROLLINS, d/o **MOSES ROLLINS**. She alive
age 60 in 1850 census. Living with son Paul T.
Occ. farmer and cooper. Res. Barnstead, N.H.
[NHVS][Barrington T.R.] 1830 census at
Strafford.

Children: 183. **PAUL T.**, b. 1810, md. 4 May
      1836 **ABIGAIL OTIS**.
    184. **MARTHA**, b. 1812, d.y.
    185. **BENJAMIN F.**, b. c1816, d. 30
      Oct. 1892, ae 77-2, md. **CYNTHIA**
      G. KIMBALL. No issue.
    186. **WILLIAM M.**, b. 1815, d. unmd.
    187. **ABIGAIL A.**, b. c1818, md. 16
      June 1842 **CHARLES CLYDE** of
      Derry, NH.
    188. **DAVID B.**, b. 1822, d.y.
    189. **HOLMAN ROLLINS**, b. 1824, d.y.

91. **WILLIAM WINKLEY [WILLIAM 44]** He was born 13
Jan. 1789 at Barrington, NH and died there 23
May 1866, ae 77 a widower [NHVR]. He married
26 Nov. 1817 at Dover **SARAH HUSSEY** d/o **RICHARD
HUSSEY.** She born 1794 and died 10 Jan. 1862 at
Barrington, NH, ae 67-6. Both buried William
Waterhouse Cem., Barrington. His will dated 22
Apr. 1863, proved June 1866. [#2677] [Dover
Hist. Coll.]

Child: 190. **MARTHA A.**, b. 9 Nov. 1819, d.
            18 Jan. 1894, md. 29 Sep. 1841
            JEREMIAH WATERHOUSE Jr., by
            Rev. Francis V. Pike of
            Rochester. Had: **WILLIAM E.** b.
            31 Jan. 1845, d. 20 Nov. 1902,
            md. **ELIZABETH HALE.**

94. **ANN WINKLEY [WILLIAM 44]** She born 27 Jan.
1796 at Barrington and died 11 Dec. 1871. She
married 9 July 1822 **JEREMIAH BUGGELL** at Durham.
[NHVR] [Straff. Co. md., 53] He died 2 July
1853, ae 62 yrs. Children named Buggell:

Children: i. **MARTHA W.** b. 27 Mar. 1823, d. 29
                Nov. 1909, md. **Dr. WILLIAM
                WATERHOUSE.** 1815-1907.
            ii. **JOHN J.**, d. 26 June 1857 age
                31 yrs, md. **SARAH TUTTLE.**
           iii. **MARY**, b. 12 Nov. 1825.
            iv. **WILLIAM H.**, b. 23 June 1829.
             v. **MARK F.**, b. 26 Nov. 1831, d.
                1835.
            vi. **CHARLES F.**, b. 20 Feb. 1837.

97. **SAMUEL WINKLEY [WILLIAM 44]** He was born 5
Oct. 1805 at Barrington, NH and died 17 Apr.
1863, age 57 yrs. [NH Bible Rec. 314] He
married 1st at Barrington 28 Dec. 1828 **NANCY
FOSS**, d/o **SAMUEL & BETSY (BABB) FOSS.** [NHVR] She
born 13 May 1808 and died 20 Mar. 1836 [27y.].
He married 2nd 12 Mar. 1839 **LYDIA FOYE** of Dover,
N.H. She born c1805 and died 28 Oct. 1881 [77y.]
[NHVR] Children by 2nd wife. In 1830 - 1850
census. Occ. farmer. Res. at Barrington, NH.

Children: 191. **MARY E.**, b. 13 Oct. 1840.
        192. **ABBIE V.**, b. 18 Nov. 1844.

98. **JOANNA WINKLEY [WILLIAM 44]** She born 13 Dec. 1810 and died 8 June 1857 at Rochester, NH. She married 7 June 1829 **WILLIAM HAYES Esq.** of Rochester, NH. Children named Hayes:

Children: i. **WILLIAM WINKLEY**, b. 24 May 1830.
      ii. **GEORGE LAFAYETTE**, b. 5 Dec. 1831. d. 23 July 1854.
     iii. **MARY JOAN**, b. 24 June 1834.
     iv. **ALBERT WATSON**, b. 27 Nov. 1836.
      v. **ANGELINE**, b. 26 Mar. 1839.
     vi. **ORVILL HENRY**, b. 4 June 1844.
    vii. **NORMAN PARIS**, b. 9 July 1849.

100. **DANIEL WINKLEY [JOHN 45]** He was born 26 May 1792 at Strafford and died there 4 Feb. 1883. He married 20 Mar. 1816 **SARAH OTIS**, d/o **Hon. JOB & SALLY (KIMBALL) OTIS**. She b. 31 Mar. 1798 and died 13 Mar. 1886, ae 87-11-13. Moved to Oxford, N.H. 1824 - 1837 Strafford and 1857 Malden, Mass. Selectman, General Court 1836. Member Free Baptist Church. In 1830 & 1840 census at Rochester. His mother lived with them in 1850 census. Occ. farmer. [NH Gen. Digest, p.272, Glenn Towle 1986] [Hist. of Rock. Co.] [NH Gazetteer 3:47] [NEHGR 5:218]

Children: 193. **OTIS PLUMMER**, b. 25 Oct. 1816, d. 22 Sep. 1896, unmd. Farmer.
      194. **JOHN A.**, [NH Gen. Rec. 1:151]
      195. **DANIEL SWAIN**,

101. **Rev. JOHN WINKLEY [JOHN 45]** He was born 29 Jan. 1797 or 1 Feb. 1795 at Barrington, NH and died 19 Oct. 1868, ae 73-8-18 at Stafford, NH. He married 9 Nov. 1815 by Rev. Enoch Place **SUSAN OTIS** d/o **STEPHEN & HANNAH (EMERSON) OTIS**. She b. 3 Jan. 1793 and died 4 Jan. 1873, at Strafford, NH ae 83-0-1. [NEHGR 5:221] He was ordained at Durham 4 Sep. 1825. Buried Strafford Cemetery. Res. Crown Point Road, Strafford, N.H. Occ. farmer. In 1850 census. [NEHGR 76:28][Gen. Rec. Straff. Co., v18, #6, p.91] Church elder.

Children: 196. JEREMIAN S., b. 8 Nov. 1816, d.
            17 Mar. 1906, md. 26 Feb. 1835
            BETSY HILL.

102. **SAMUEL WINKLEY [JOHN 45]** He married **NANCY FIFIELD.** She born 1794. They moved to Plainfield, NH.

Children: 197. **ALONZO K.**, b. c1822, md. 19
            June 1841 **ELIZABETH J.
            DANIOLES.** In 1850 census. No
            children.
            198. **MARY A.**, poss. md. c1841 **MARTIN
            COLE.**

103. **SWAIN WINKLEY [JOHN 45]** He was born 11 Jan. 1802 at Cambridge. He married **HARRIET HAMMOND.** She born 1817 in Maine. In 1850 census at Malden, Mass. Occ. tailer.

Children: 199. **MARY A.**, b. 1845.
            200. **MARIA**, b. 1848.

104. **DAVID WINKLEY [JOHN 45]** He was born c1810. He married **MARIA LEWIS** at Boston. She born c1810. Occ. tailor. In 1850 census at Concord, NH. His will dated 18 Dec. 1848, proved 4 Jan. 1855.

Children: 201. **SARAH M.**, b. c1835.

107. **SAMUEL WINKLEY [BENJ. 47]** He was born 25 Nov. 1797 or 1798 at Barrington, N.H. and died 24 Oct. 1872 age 75 at Barnstead. [NHVS] He married 7 Jan. 1827 **MARY MARTIN,** d/o **JOHN MARTIN** at Amesbury, Mass. She died 3 May 1883, ae 83-7. Res. Barnstead, N.H. Occ. farmer. In 1830 census.

Children: 205. **JEFFERSON M.**, md. 12 July 1860
            REBECCA D. CHAMBERLAIN, Auburn,
            Maine.
            206. **ALONZO,** md. **ELIZA DANIEL.**

108. **BENJAMIN WINKLEY Jr.** [BENJ. 46] He was born 1 Feb. 1800 at Dover. He married 23 Nov. 1826 **ELIZA C. HOIT** of Newmarket, N.H. Occ. lawyer at Exeter, NH. She died at Exeter Nov. 1832, ae 30 yrs. [NHGR 6:34]

Children: i. DAU, b. July 1830.
          ii. DAU., b. 26 July 1832.

109. **MEHITABLE WINKLEY** [BENJAMIN 47] She born 24 June 1802. She married 24 Nov. 1824 Capt. **JOHN FELKER** of Barnstead, NH. Res. Barrington, NH. Children named FELKER:

Children: i. ISAAC C.,   vi. JOHN W.,
           ii. SARAH J.,   vii. BENJAMIN F.,
          iii. ELIZABETH,   viii. CHAS. FREEMAN,
           iv. WILLIAM H.,   ix. AUGUSTUS A.,
            v. MARY S.,   x. ROXANNA A.,

110. **EBENEZER P. WINKLEY** [BENJ. 47] He was born 12 Oct. 1804 at Barnstead and died 14 Mar. 1870 at Concord, N.H. age 65-5. He married 14 Sep. 1836 at Lowell, Mass. **ELIZA WARREN WHITCOMB**, d/o **PAUL & SALLY (SAMPSON) WHITCOMB**. She born 21 Apr. 1816 at Waterford, Me. and died 31 Jan. 1896 at Berwick, Me. age 79-10-21. [NHVS] Both buried at Concord, N.H. She married second 24 Dec. 1882 **MARK MARDEN**. [NHVR] Occ. machinist and cabinet maker. Census 1840 Middlesex Co., MA, 1850 & 1860 Concord, NH. Ward 7. [Lowell MA VS p.316, 396 & 404]

Children: 210. **WILLIAM WARREN**, b. 7 Oct. 1839,
                at Lowell, MA, d. 8 Nov. 1844.
                (5-1-1) at Concord, NH.
           211. **GEORGE WASHINGTON**, b. 16 Jan.
                1846, d. 22 May 1924, md. 31
                Mar. 1866 **NANCY W. BAKER**.
           212. **SARAH ELIZABETH**, b. 1852, md. 7
                June 1875 **LEWIS A. GUPTILL**. 6
                children.
           213. **CHARLES E./EBEN P.**, b. 1857, d.
                13 Jan. 1937, d.s.p.

111. **FRANCIS WINKLEY** [BENJAMIN 47] He was born 2 Mar. 1807 at Barnstead, NH and died 1849 at Barnstead, NH. He married 1832 **OLIVE HANNIFORD**. She born 1800 and died 1851.

Children: 220. OLIVE F., b. 1849, d. 1854.
221. MARY A., d. 1844.

113. **WILLIAM PLUMMER WINKLEY** [BENJAMIN 47] He was born 26 May 1816 and died 26 Jan. 1899. He probably married at Springfield, Mass. 25 Sep. 1842 **HELEN M. SIMONS**. He m.2, at Epsom, NH 1 Jan. 1852 **MARY A. DOLBEER**. Res. at Chicopee, Mass.

115. **DAVID B. WINKLEY** [BENJAMIN 47] He born 18 Sep. 1821 at Barnstead, NH and died a widower at Stafford 9 Feb. 1908. He married 23 Jan. 1848 **MARY S. WEEKS** d/o **ELISHA & MARY (POTTER) WEEKS**, by Rev. Enoch Place. [NEHGR 76:91] She born 6 Oct. 1825 died 20 Apr. 1903. Both buried at Berwick, Maine. 1850 census at Rollingsford. Occ. mfr.

121. **FRANCIS WINKLEY** [MARK H. 50] He was born 22 Mar. 1797 at Barrington, N.H. and died 18 Nov. 1862. He married 18 April 1822 **SARAH NOBLE (SALLY)**, d/o **WILLIAM PITT & REBECCA (BUNKER) LOUGEE** of Strafford. She born 24 Apr. 1796 and died 23 Oct. 1881. Occ. farmer. Res. Strafford and Alton, N.H. In 1850 census at Alton.

Children: 240. **TAMSON HAYES**, b. 2 Apr. 1824, md. **JOHN P. CLOUGH** of Gilmonton Iron Works, NH
241. **ABBIE P.**, b. 1833, md. **WILLIAM J. FOSS**, 3 children.
242. **REBECCA/EMMA LOUGEE**, d. 5 Dec. 1895, md. **BENJAMIN P. MARSTON**.
243. **JOHN HUNKING**, b. 20 Feb. 1823, moved to Minn. md. 1 Sep. 1844 **HANNAH NUTTER LOUGEE** at Manchester. N.H.
244. **WILLIAM PITT**, b. 9 Feb. 1829, d. 20 July 1910, md. 23 Jan. 1855 **SUSANNAH CHOWEN**.

122. **MARTHA WINKLEY [MARK H. 50]** She born 1800 and died 1863. She married **JOHN PERKINS** of Strafford, NH. He born 1797 and died 1873. Children named Perkins:

Children: i. **TAMSON B.**, b. 1824, d. 1826.
   ii. **PAUL Jr.**, b. 1829, d. 1919, md. **MARY J. PERKINS.**
   iii. **WARREN**, b. 1832, d. 1910, md. **NANCY L. FOSS.**
   iv. **MARY H.**, b. 1835, d. 1853.

123. **PAUL WINKLEY [MARK H. 50]** He was born 3 Feb. 1803 at Stafford, NH and died there 15 Aug. 1870. He married 29 Nov. 1821 **LYDIA MILLETT JONES**, d/o **WILLIAM JONES**. She born 11 Nov. 1804 and died 15 April 1891. Paul divorced 21 June 1866 on grounds of abandonment and refusal to co-habit. Daughter ADELINE LEIGHTON was executrix of his estate. Perkins cem. at Stafford, NH. Occ. farmer in 1850 census.

Children: 250. **MARTHA**, md. 28 May 1862 **JOHN DREW FOSS**, s/o **SIMON & SARAH (BECK) FOSS**. Had: **HIRAM**.
   251. **WILLIAM M.**, b. Mar. 1824, md. 10 Mar. 1847 **DEBORAH BROOKS**.
   252. **MARK HUNKING Jr.**, b. 15 Oct. 1825, d. 12 Aug. 1867, md. 2 Oct. 1850 **SALLY F. LEIGHTON**.
   253. **ADELINE**, b. 24 Mar. 1827, d. 2 Aug. 1894, md. 18 Oct. 1846 **SAMUEL LEIGHTON**.
   254. **LOVEY A.**, b. 31 July 1832, d. 21 Mar. 1899, md. 14 Sep. 1852 **TRUEWORTHY LEIGHTON**. 5 ch.
   255. **JOHN S.**, b. 1836, d. 16 Mar. 1888 [51-10-18] md. 29 Nov. 1862 **DEBORAH H. BERRY**.
   256. **PAUL HAYES Jr**, b. 15 Feb. 1835, d. 16 Feb. 1920, md. **BELINDA J. HOLMES**.
   257. **CLARISSE**, b. 1839, d. 2 Nov. 1876, md. **DAVID M. PERKINS**. 2 children.
   258. **ELIZA J.**, b. c1846, md. _____ **BLOOD**. No ch.

124. DENNIS WINKLEY [MARK H. 50] He was born 1809 and died 20 June 1889 [79-7-24] at Strafford, NH. He married 7 Apr. 1831 MARY A. HOWARD, d/o WILLIAM & POLLY (HANSON) HOWARD at Stafford. She born c1813 and died 17 July 1886, ae 73. Occ. farming. Had 90 acre farm. In 1840 - 1860 census. He died intestate [Strafford Co. Probate #6821] Res. Stafford, N.H.

He was appointed guardian on 5 July 1865 to MARY FRANCES & EMMA WINKLEY children of GEORGE WINKLEY of Pittsfield, NH. Both under age 14 yrs. (Straff. Co. Probate #2522) In 1850 census,

Children: 260. GEORGE, b. c1831, d. by 1881.
            261. EMILY H., b. c1833, m.1, 6 Oct.
                 1855 ISAAC P. McMASTER, m.2,
                 _____ WORTHAM.
            262. MERCY, b. 6 Aug. 1835, d. 27
                 Jan. 1929 AT Manchester, NH.
            263. MARTHA J., b. c1837, md. EUGENE
                 REED.
            264. BETSY A., b. c1839, d. by 1881,
                 md. _____ CLOUGH.
            265. MARQUIS D., b. c1841, d. c1871.
            266. MARY E., b. c1844, md. FRED JOY
            267. ELLEN F., b. c1846.
            268. HERBERT C., b. 7 Mar. 1849, d.
                 15 Sep. 1927, md. c1877
                 ELIZABETH A. TILTON.
            269. ELLA T., b. 28 May 1851, md.
                 CHARLES TUCKER.
            270. JASON W., b. c1856, d. 25 Apr.
                 1894, md. 1 July 1883 CLARA J.
                 STRAW.
            271. ADA W., b. c1858, md. 4 Sep.
                 1879 CLARENCE E. FRANK.
            272. MARY E., b. c1860, 1870 Census
                 Poss. d/o George Winkley,
            273. EMMA E., b. c1862. (same)

130. ASA WINKLEY [JOHN 52] He was born 19 Dec. 1801 and died 27 June 1854. He married 29 Jan. 1828 HANNAH WINGATE d/o JONATHAN WINGATE of Madbury, N.H. Named in 1830 census at Barrington. She born 1801 at Madbury and died 12 Oct. 1841, ae 40 at Dover. They lived at Barrington, NH. In 1840 census.

Children: 275. JEREMIAH OTIS/OETO, b. 5 Feb.
1830, md. 3 Aug. 1854 FRANCES
CAROLINE NUTTER.
276. FRANCIS STEPHENS, b. 1832.
277. JOHN S., b. 1838, d. 1883, md.
1868 ROSILAH REED. (1842-1923)

132. JOHN HUNKING WINKLEY Jr. [JOHN 52] He born
14 Aug. 1805 at Barrington, NH died 27 May 1878
[72-10] He married 1st, 2 Mar. 1835 KEZIAH Y.
BROCK. She died 7 Feb. 1850 [39-6] He married
2nd 1 Apr. 1851 SUSAN Y. BROCK d/o ISAAC & POLLY
(YOUNG) BROCK. She died 22 Apr. 1894, ae 79-3-
13. His will dated 14 May 1878, proved 1 June
1878. Wife named executrix [Strafford Co.
probate #4695]

Children: 280. ARTEMISIA CLEMENTIA, b. 3 May
1836, d. 28 Oct. 1837 [1-5-4].
281. MELVILLE LASSELL, b. 11 Nov.
1837, d. 15 June 1867.
282. ALMA LANDALL LAFEYETTE, b. 26
Sep. 1842, d. 14 Sep. 1866.
283. JOHN VINAL LEGREND, b. 28 May
1844, d. 12 Sep. 1846 [2-3-0]
284. ATAZINE MYRANETTE, b. 5 Mar.
1847, m.1, 29 July 1891 HENRY
H. WOODBURY, m.2, HIRAM H.
LUFLER. (Poss. daughter)
285. JOHN NICHOLAS, b. 1848.
Children by 2nd wife:
287. ABIEL CLINTON, d.y.
288. CHARLES FRANKLIN, b. 19 Dec.
1854, d. 15 Dec. 1923, md.
LAURA L. d/o HATEVILLE &
ELIZABETH (HENDERSON) BUMFORD.
Divorced 5 Sep. 1877. She
died 2 May 1926, He m.2, 19
Mar. 1895 Mrs. ZOE
(BOURQUE) COLT.

133. JEREMIAH WINKLEY [JOHN 52] He was born 8
July 1807 and died 16 July 1891, ae 84 at
Barrington, NH. He married 2 Oct. 1831 MARY JANE
LANGLEY at Lee, NH. [Lowell, MA V.R.] Occ.
millwright. In 1840 census. 1850 census at
Newmarket, NH.

Children: 290. **MARTHA**, b. 1832.
             291. **MERCE?**, b. 1833.
             292. **CHARLES**, b. 1834.
             293. **E___LEA?** (m), b. 1837.
             294. **GEORGE**, b. 1840.
             295. **OREN**, b. 1842.

135. **JOHN HUNKING WINKLEY** [FRANCIS 54] He was born 8 Feb. 1800 and died 1872 at Barrington, NH. He married 21 Mar. 1841 **ELIZA** d/o **CONSTANTINE & ABIGAIL CHOATE** of Lowell, MA. She born 10 Apr.1815 at Enfield, NH. and died 27 May 1878 (72-10-0) [AF]

Children: 300. **JOHN LANGDON**, b. 10 Mar. 1841,
                  d. 16 Dec. 1888 [age 46], md.
                  ELLEN S. YOUNG.
             301. **ISABEL**, b. 1845.
             302. **FLORANCE**, md. **GEORGE SMITH**.
             303. **WILLIAM C.**, d. 20 Jan. 1847.
             304. **DAVID C.**, d. 14 July 1847,
                  0-0-1.
             305. **SARAH M.**, b. 1849, md. **ALBERT
                  NICHOLSON**.
             306. **GEORGE C.**, b. 1851, md.
                  FLORANCE COOK.
             307. **FRANK D.**, b. 1855.
             308. **ELIZABETH R.**, b. 1858.

138. **DARIUS WINKLEY** [FRANCIS 54] He was born 17 June 1807 and died 17 Mar. 1864 at Barrington, NH. He married 1st 31 Oct. 1841 **URSULA R. HALL** d/o **JOSEPH & MARY (SHANNON) HALL** at Barnstead, NH. She born 17 Aug. 1811 and died 1844. He married 2nd **MARIA DANIELS**. She born 1821 and died 1847. He married 3rd 24 Mar. 1851 at Dover **SARAH McDUFFEE CATE** of Dover, NH. She born 1818 and died 1891 at Barrington, N.H. Children by 3rd wife: 1850 census. He died intestate [Strafford Co. Probate #2296]. Occ. clothier. Owned 80 acre farm. Had interest in sawmill.

Children: 309. Infant daughter, d. 10 July
                  1842.
             310. **DARIUS D.**, b. 1847.

311. **URSULA MARIA**, b. 25 Dec. 1850,
md. 12 Nov. 1878 **ENOCH OSBORN
TASKER.**
312. **JOSEPH CATE**, b. 13 Dec. 1853,
d. 7 Feb. 1934.
313. **CYRUS A.**, b. 1853, d. 1855.
314. **CHARLES W.**, b. 1858, d. 1863.

141. **JOSEPH WINKLEY** [FRANCIS 54] He was born
June 1814 at Barrington , NH. and died 30 Oct.
1890 at Dover, NH [74-4-24]. He married 11 Apr.
1841 at Dover **MARY "POLLY" CATER.** She born
c1829. His will dated 6 Aug. 1881, proved 5 Nov.
1890. [Strafford Co. Probate #7226]. Occ. farmer
res. at Dover, NH In 1850 census.

Children: 320. **LUCINDA A.**, b. c1842, d. by 6
Aug. 1881.
321. **MARY F.**, b. c1844, d. by 6 Aug.
1881, md. 26 Mar. 1868 **JOHN C.
TASKER.**
322. **JOHN FRANK**, b. 5 Feb. 1846, d.
30 Oct. 1908, md. 9 July 1870
LUCINDA LADD.

150. **WILLIAM WINKLEY** [JOSEPH W. 65] He was born
c1807 in Ohio. He married **SUSAN KNICKENBOCKER.**
She born 1825 in NY. Res. York twp. Guilford,
Dearborn Co., Indiana. [AF] At Aurora in 1850
census.

Children: 325. **MARION/MARY**, b. 20 June 1845,
md. **JOHN FULLER.**
326. **THOMAS BENTON**, b. 20 Mar. 1847,
d. 9 Dec. 1910, md. 10 Feb.
1869 **SARAH MARTHA ROBERTS.**
327. **CHARLES PEARSON**, b. 1849, md.
23 Oct. 1872 **MARY ALICE HIGBEE.**
328. **CLARA**, b. 1851, md. **ROY WILBUR.**

151. **JOSEPH WENDECKER WINKLEY** [JOSEPH W. 65] He
was born 1812 in Ohio and died 5 Apr. 1857. He
married c1831 **ELIZABETH** _____. She born c1814 in
KY. Res. Dearborn Co., Indiana. In 1850 census
at Aurora.

Children: 329. **LEWIS**, b. 1833, blacksmith.
             330. **EDSON S.**, b. 1835.
             331. **ANDREW S.**, b. 1848.

153. **JOHN L. WINKLEY** [**JOSEPH W.** 65] He was born
c1816 in Indiana? Had wife **HARRIET** born 1821 in
Ohio. In Centre Twp, Dearborn Co., Ind. in 1850
census.

Children: 340. **RICHARD**, b. 1840.
             341. **SARAH J.**, b. 1841.
             342. **JAMES**, b. 1845.
             343. **ANNA**, b. 1846.
             344. **ESAL**, b. 1850.

155. **JOHN B. WINKLEY** [unknown] He was born 1804
in Vt. Had wife **HARRIET** born 1804 in NH. Occ.
farmer. In 1850 census at Bridgeport, Vt. Not in
1840 Vt. census.

Children: 350. **SUSAN**, b. 1831.
             351. **OLEAN?**, b. 1833.
             352. **ABRAHAM**, b. 1834.
             353. **HELEN**, b. 1838.
             354. **CLARK**, b. 1840.
             355. **JOHN**, b. 1843.
             356. **ANNE**, b. 1847.

SIXTH GENERATION

159. JOHN F. WINKLEY [JOHN 71] He was born 17
Mar. 1817 at Portsmouth, NH. He married 3 Feb.
1850 CAROLINE , d/o Capt. ROBERT LEFAVOUR.
Clergyman P.E. Church. [Amer. Anc. 5:60]

160. SAMUEL HOBART WINKLEY [JOHN 71] he was born
5 April 1819 and died 1 August 1911 at Dublin,
N.H. He married 13 August 1849 MARTHA WELLINGTON
PARKER, d/o WILLIAM & MARTHA (WELLINGTON) PARKER
of Boston, Mass. She born 13 August 1826 and
died 8 Jan. 1912 at Boston. Grad. of Harvard.

Children: 490. MARTHA PARKER, b. 12 Aug. 1850,
            d. 16 Apr. 1933, md. 29 Sep.
            1875 Major CHARLES RUSSELL
            SUTER, U.S. Army. 6 children.

183. PAUL T. WINKLEY [PAUL T. 90] He was born
1810 at Barnstead or at Barrington, N.H.   He
married 4 May 1836 ABIGAIL K. OTIS d/o Hon.
NATHANIEL & MARIA H. OTIS of Strafford by Rev.
Enoch Place. [NEHGR 5:218, 76:38]. She b. 1809
in NH and d. 1877. Res. Newbury, Mass. Occ.
farmer. In 1850 census.

Children: 494. ABBY AUGUSTA, b. 4 Nov. 1839.
            495. SARAH MARIA, b. 30 Oct. 1842.
            496. JOB OTIS, b. 26 Feb. 1844.
            497. MARY GARAFILIA, b. 7 Feb. 1846
            498. VIOLA FRANCES, b. 21 Aug. 1848.
            499. PAUL T.,

187. ABIGAIL WINKLEY [PAUL T. 90] She born
c1818. She married 16 June 1842 CHARLES CLYDE
of Derry, NH. Children named CLYDE.

Children: i. MARTHA J.   iii. CHARLES M.
            ii. MARIA A.   iv. BENJAMIN F.

196. JEREMIAH S. WINKLEY [JOHN 101] He was born
8 Nov. 1816 at Barrington, NH and died 17 Mar.
1906 [89-4-9] at Dover, NH. He married 26 Feb.
1835 ELIZABETH HILL, d/o JOSEPH & BETSY

(HANSON) HILL. [NEHGR 5:221] She born 12 July
1816 and died 8 May 1900. Res. Strafford, N.H.
Buried Stafford Corner cem.

Children: 500. JOHN H., b. 1835, d. 9 Aug.
                 1863. (ae 28-1-15)
            501. STEPHEN O., b. 1838, d. 13 Nov.
                 1841 (3-9-21).
            502. LAVINA, b. 1840, md. poss. 31
                 May 1857 SAMUEL D. BERRY.
            503. MARIA L., b. c1843, md. 2
                 Nov. 1862 CHARLES M. JEWELL.
                 [NEHGR 76:44]
            504. DANIEL S., b. 1845, d. 14 Sep.
                 1853 (8-6-2)
            505. JOSEPH A., b. 14 Aug. 1847, d.
                 2 May 1936, md. 9 Nov. 1868
                 MARY E. BABB.
            506. CHRYSTINA M., b. 1850, d. 22
                 Sep. 1853 (3-5-20)
            507. ELISA J., b. 1853, md. 16 Oct.
                 1872 HIRAM A. BERRY.
            508. ABBIE J., b. 1856, md. 1892
                 WILLIAM J. FOSS.

206. ALONZO WINKLEY [SAMUEL 107] He married
ELIZABETH d/o JOHN DANIEL of Mendon, MA. She
born 7 July 1823. Settled in Iowa. [NEHGR
55:321]

Children: 510. MARY ANN, b. 21 Mar. 1860.

211. GEORGE WASHINGTON WINKLEY [EBENEZER P. 110]
He was born 14 Jan. 1846 at Lowell, Mass. and
died 22 May 1924, 4019 Warwick Ave. in Chicago,
Ill. [Cook Co. Cert. #14,334-17] He married 31
Mar. 1866 NANCY W. BAKER at Epsom, N.H. d/o
WILLIAM M. & SARAH J. (TRIPP) BAKER. She was
born 2 Dec. 1838 at Loudon, N.H. and died 10
Jan. 1905 at Hopedale, Mass. Occ. carriage
maker. 1870 census Concord, NH Ward #7. Both
buried in Vernon Grove Cem. at Milford, Mass.

Children: 530. FRANK H., b. Dec. 1868, d. Feb.
                1941, md. MARY DAWSON.

531. **EVELYN M.**, b. 5 Oct. 1872, d.
17 June 1916, md. 3 Oct. 1898
ALFRED DANIEL YEATON. 3 ch.
[authors grandparents]
532. **ALICE MAUD**, b. 21 Aug. 1876, d.
17 Oct. 1942, md. 1 Sep. 1896
ERWIN KIBBY. 2 children.
533. **G. EDWARD**, b. Apr. 1875, md.
Mrs. **MAUD** _____.

212. **SARAH ELIZABETH WINKLEY** [EBENEZER P. 110]
She was born 1852. She married 7 June 1875 **LEWIS
A. GUPTILL** s/o **GRANVILLE & BETSY (RICKER)
GUPTILL**. He born 15 Apr. 1854. Occ. carpenter.
Had 6 children. three living in 1896. [NHVS]

243. **JOHN HUNKING WINKLEY** [FRANCIS 121] He was
born 20 Feb. 1823. He married 1 Sep. 1844 **HANNAH
NUTTER LOUGEE** d/o **SAMUEL LOUGEE** of Manchester,
N.H. They moved to Fairbault, Minn. Occ. seaman
before moving to Minn. [Rice Co. Historian,
v.12, Iss. 4, Oct. 1984][NEHGR 118:190]

Children: 535. **ALBERT**, Owned Winkley Livery
                  Stables.
             536. **EMMA**, school teacher.

244. **WILLIAM PITT WINKLEY** [FRANCIS 121] He was
born 9 Feb. 1829 in Strafford, NH and died 20
July 1901 at Java, S.D. He married 23 Jan. 1855
at Downie, Ontario, Canada **SUSANNAH CHOWEN**. She
born 8 Sep. 1836 in Devon, England and died 9
Feb. 1906 at Java, S.D. Moved to Michigan and
next homestead at Fairbault, MN with bro. JOHN
(#243). Occ. iron worker. In 1886 homesteaded in
Dakota Terr. near Java. Had 6 children. [NEHGR
118:189] He had a machine shop and foundry. Had
a meat market at Java. [All Our Yesterdays, Nora
Winkley, 1982]

Children: 537. **FRANCIS/FRANK CHOWEN**, b. 3 Sep.
                  1864, d. 28 Feb. 1956, md. 20
                  Feb. 1886 **NORA MARY ROBINSON**.

Note: Either John or Wm Pitt was probably father
of **FLORETTE ESTELLE WINKLEY** who md. 3 Jan. 1874
MILEM L. HAMMETT at Fairbault, Minn.

251. **WILLIAM M. WINKLEY** [PAUL 123] He was born
Mar. 1824 at Barrington, NH. He married 10 Mar.
1847 **DEBORAH BROOKS**. Served Union Army in Civil
War. At Dover, NH in 1850 census. Occ. farmer.
Moved to Clearfield, Taylor County, Iowa.

Children: 538. **ISORA E.**, b. 1849.
             539. **FRANK**, b. 1855.
             540. **FLORA**, b. 1859.

252. **MARK HUNKING Jr.** [PAUL 123] He was born 15
Oct. 1825 at Barrington, NH and died 12 Aug.
1867. He married 2 Oct. 1850 **SALLY FOSS
LEIGHTON**, d/o **ISAAC & ABIGAIL (DREW) LEIGHTON**.
She born c1830 and died 22 Apr. 1912 [82-1-11]
at Strafford, NH. Occ. Shoemaker. Civil War 15th
Regt. NHV. Buried in Perkins Cemetery. Res.
Strafford, N.H.

Children: 541. **LYDIA ABBIE**, b. 21 Oct. 1851,
                  d. 21 Sep. 1852.
             542. **SARAH FRANCES**, b. 15 Jan. 1854,
                  md. 1875 **OSCAR ROCKWELL LOCKE**.
                  3 children.
             543. **HANNAH AMANDA**, b. 16 May 1855,
                  d. 23 Nov. 1915, md. 1873
                  GEORGE WALTER STACY. 4 ch.
             544. **MARTHA EVELYN**, b. 1 June 1857,
                  d. 19 May 1940, md. 20 June
                  1878 **ELISHA GOODWIN Jr.** 1
                  child.
             545. **FLORA IDELLA**, b. 17 June 1859,
                  d. 23 Nov. 1875, [17-5-17]
                  unmd.
             546. **MARK HENRY**, b. 23 May 1861, d.
                  21 April 1938, md. 23 May 1883
                  FLORANCE ELLA TREFETHEN.
             547. **IDA MAY (DIDA)**, b. 18 May 1863,
                  d. 4 Feb. 1917, md. 20 July
                  1885 **FRANK LINCOLN HAYES**. No ch

548. **PAUL EDGAR**, b. 6 May 1865, d.
10 Jan. 1947, md. 24 Oct. 1891
ELLA FRANCES PROCTER at Dover.

253. **ADELINE WINKLEY** [PAUL 123] She was born 24
Mar. 1827 and died 2 Aug. 1894. She married 18
Oct. 1846 **SAMUEL LEIGHTON** at Strafford, NH.
Children named LEIGHTON:

Children: i. **WILLIAM MARQUIS**, b. 2 Oct. 1846.
          ii. **STEPHEN MILLET**, b. 24 Oct. 1847.
         iii. **MARTHA FRANCINA**, b. 2 Sep. 1850.
          iv. **OLIVE ADELINE**, b. 16 Aug. 1853.
           v. **ABBIE LYDIA**, b. 13 Aug. 1855.
          vi. **IDA BELLE**, b. 16 May 1857.
         vii. **EMMA LOVELY**, b. 28 Aug. 1858.
        viii. **MARY ADA**, b. 11 Mar. 1860.

254. **LOVEY A. WINKLEY** [PAUL 123] She was born 31
July 1832 and died 21 Mar. 1899. She married 14
Sep. 1852 **TRUEWORTHY LEIGHTON** at Barnstead, NH.
Children named LEIGHTON at Strafford, NH.

Children: i. **JOHN H.**, b. c1853.
          ii. **WILLIAM A.**, b. c1855.
         iii. **EDWIN**, b. c1858.

255. **JOHN S. WINKLEY** [PAUL 123]   He was born
1836 and died 16 March 1888, age 51-10-18. He
married 29 Nov. 1862 **DEBORAH B. BERRY**, d/o **PETER
& SUSAN (BABB) BERRY** at New Durham, NH. She born
c1839 and died 8 July 1887 at North Strafford,
NH. age 49-4-25. [Strafford Co. Probate #6650 &
6651] One source says he md. **DEBORAH B. HOLMES**.
[Delmar W. Goodman]

256. **PAUL HAYES WINKLEY Jr.** [PAUL 123]   He was
born 15 Feb. 1835 and died 16 Feb. 1920 at
Tilton, NH. He married **BELINDA JANE HOLMES**, d/o
JOHN W. & BELINDA (BABB) HOLMES. She born 8 July
1850 and died 6 Dec. 1888.

Children: 550. **PAUL HERMAN (or HERMAN P.)**, b.
           1 Mar. 1874, d. 1961, md. 19
           Aug. 1908 **WINIFRED E. CHESLEY**,

551. CHARLES EUGENE, b. 22 May 1873, d. 12 July 1956, md. ?? HELEN RAYMOND.

268. HERBERT C. WINKLEY [DENNIS 124] He was born 7 Mar. 1849 and died 15 Sep. 1927 at Pittsfield, NH. He married ELIZABETH A. TILTON d/o DAVID P. & SARAH R. (BUNKER) TILTON. She born 13 Feb. 1848 at Pittsfield and died there 11 Feb. 1933. Occ. Carpenter.

Children: 555. SARAH TILTON, b. 12 Jan. 1881.

270. JASON W. WINKLEY [DENNIS 124] He was born c1856 at Strafford, NH and died 25 Apr. 1894 age 38 at Webster. He married 1 July 1883 CLARA J. STRAW at Pittsfield, NH. She divorced him on grounds of habitual drunkenness on 3 Nov. 1883.

Children: 557. SON, b. 27 June 1884.

275. JEREMIAH OTIS/ORTA WINKLEY [ASA 130] He was born 5 Feb. 1830. He married 3 August 1854 FRANCES CAROLINE NUTTER at Barnstead. Res. Parsonfield, Me.

Children: 560. JOSEPHINE AUGUSTA, b. 1 Aug.
                  1855 at Boston.
             561. LIZZIE WINGATE, b. 1 Sep. 1860.
             562. LULA FRANCES, b. 17 May 1863.

288. CHARLES FRANKLIN WINKLEY [JOHN HUNKING 132] He was born 19 Dec. 1854 at Barrington, NH and died 15 Nov. 1923 at Nottingham, NH. He married LAURA L. BUMFORD, d/o HATEVILLE & ELIZABETH (HENDERSON) BUMFORD. Divorced on grounds of desertion 5 Sep. 1877. She got custody of son. She died 2 May 1926. He married 2nd, 19 Mar. 1895 Mrs. ZOE (BOVARQUE) COLT.

Children: 570. ALTON BUMFORD, b. 30 Oct. 1877,
                  d. 15 Aug. 1926, md. 29 Nov.
                  1905 MARY E. CASSIDY, d/o
                  EDWARD & ELIZABETH (MORAN)
                  CASSIDY. She b. 1881. Occ.
                  beltmaker.

300. JOHN LANGDON WINKLEY [JOHN H. 135] He was born 10 Mar. 1841 and died 16 Dec. 1888. He married ELLEN SARAH YOUNG. Res. at Barrington, NH.

Children: 575. GRACE ELLEN, b. 26 June 1873.
            576. LILLIAN ABBIE, b. 1 Jan. 1877.
            577. GEORGE LANGDON, b. 31 Jan. 1879.
            578. WILLARD CHOATE, b. 1 June 1885.

322. JOHN FRANK WINKLEY [JOSEPH 141] He was born 5 Feb. 1846 at Dover, NH and died 30 Oct. 1908. He married 9 July 1870 LUCINDA LADD, d/o JOHN & LUCINDA LADD at Dover, NH. She born 8 Nov. 1849 at Saco, Maine.

Children: 580. ALTA G., b. 2 Feb. 1873, d. 17 Sep. 1900.
            581. Daughter, b. 26 Aug. 1874.

326. THOMAS BENTON WINKLEY [WILLIAM 150] He was born 20 Mar. 1847 at Laughery Creek, Ind. and died 9 Apr. 1910 at Guilford, Dearborn Co., Ind. He married 10 Feb. 1869 SARAH MARTHA, d/o CHARLES E. & SUSAN (FALLIS) ROBERTS. She born 12 Apr. 1852 in Riply Co., Ind. and died 14 May 1913 at Guilford, Indiana.

Children: 600. CHARLES EDWARD, b. 14 Nov. 1869, d. 6 Sep. 1893.

400. JOHN WINKLEY [unknown] He was born 20 May 1821 in Mass. and died 2 Oct. 1897 at Point Pleasant, Mason Co., W. Va. He married 24 Oct. 1847 MARIA VIRGINIA, d/o THOMAS RICHARD & ANN (JOHNSON) FOWLER. She born 16 Oct. 1828 in Mason Co., W. Va. and died 24 Dec. 1899. Occ. engineer. He moved first to Ohio and to Mason Co. about 1840. Served in Virginia Militia. Conn. 7 Sep. 1850. Only 3 children survived childhood. Name in 1820 census in Meigs Co. and in 1830 census in Fairfield Co., Ohio. 1850 census in Mason Co. [Detroit Soc. of Gen. Res. Mag. v.30, p. 20, Fall 1966]

Reportedly one of 4 brothers. One was **CHARLES WINKLEY** a newspaper editor at Jackson, Miss. Other brothers might have been **EDWARD** and **FRANK**.

Children: 610. **ADA OHIO,**
611. **BADA ARIZONIA,**
612. **HARRIET VIRGINIA,** b. 1850, d. 1919, md. 1866 **ROBERT KIGER.** 4 children.

SEVENTH GENERATION

505. JOSEPH A. WINKLEY [JEREMIAH S. 196] He was
born 14 Aug. 1847 at Northwoods, NH and died 2
May 1936 [88-8-18] at Strafford. He married 5
Nov. 1868 **MARY E.** BABB, d/o **ASAHEL & LYDIA
(BERRY) BABB** at Strafford. She born 1836 and
died 3 June 1920 [88-8-18]. Occ. farmer and
shoemaker. Buried Crown Point Cem. Res.
Strafford, N.H. In 1870 census.

Children: 1000. **LEROY A.**, b. 1869, md. 23 Dec.
1892 **JENNIE B. GRAY.**
1001. **LILLIAN MAY**, b. 2 Jan. 1873,
md. 23 June 1894 **CHARLES H.
LEACH** at Dover, NH.
1002. **JOHN F.**, b. 4 Dec. 1875, d.
1938, m.1, **BERTHA HOWARD**,
1875-1899, m.2, 5 Feb. 1902
CORA M. HALL d/o **BENJ. &
MELLISSA (BROWN) HALL**, 1877-
1957.
1003. **FRANK B.** or **BENJ. F.**, b. 1877,
d. 1951, md. 5 May 1904 **BERTHA
(HOWARD) HORNE.**
1004. **JEREMIAH S.**, b. 10 Feb. 1879,
d. 1940, m.1, 27 Jan. 1900
VIRA EMERSON.
1005. **HIRAM A.**, b. 6 Mar. 1882, d.
1942, md. 8 May 1907 **CARRIE B.
PRESTON** d/o **ALBERT D. PRESTON.**
Had: **FORREST.**
1006. **CHARLES H.**, d. 1 May 1886, 0-
2-6.
1007. **ROSCOE ELMER**, b. 18 May 1889,
md. 15 Jan. 1910 **EUNICE E.
VARNEY**, d/o **J. FRED & EVA
(FOSS) VARNEY.** She b. 1891.

531. **EVELYN MAY WINKLEY** [GEORGE W. 211] She was
born 5 Oct. 1872 at Boston, Mass. and died 17
June 1916 in Milwaukee, WI. and is buried there
in Forest Home Cemetery. She married 3 Oct. 1898
at Hopedale, Mass. **ALFRED DANIEL**, s/o **DANIEL**

TOWLE & ANN (ROWELL) YEATON of Epsom, NH. He born 5 Mar. 1874 and died 22 Oct. 1956 at Exeter, NH. He buried at Epsom, NH. Children named Yeaton:

Children: i. **GLADYS EVELYN**, b. 13 May 1901, d. 28 Mar. 1991, md. 14 Apr. 1925 **JAMES HASLET JONES**. He born 1 Mar. 1901 and d. 13 Dec. 1991. Both buried Epsom, NH. Authors parents.
           ii. **DORIS M.**, b. 18 May 1906, md. Sep. 1936 **CHARLES W. ROTH**. 2 ch.
          iii. **MARGARET A.**, b. 3 Sep. 1907, d. 10 Nov. 1929, unmd. Buried Hinsdale, Ill.

532. **ALICE MAUD WINKLEY** [GEORGE W. 211] She was born 21 Aug. 1876 and died 17 Oct. 1942 in Chicago, Ill. She married 1 Sep. 1896 **ERWIN KIBBY**. He b. 14 Jan. 1875 and d. 24 Aug. 1940 in Chicago. Res. Chicago. Ill. Children named Kibby:

Children: i. **CLARENCE E.**, b. 16 Dec. 1897, d. May 1964, md 19 Oct. 1918 **ALBERTA W. TAUTKEN**.
           ii. **MILDRED E.**, b. 21 Jan. 1900, d. 25 Mar. 1958, md. twice. m.2, 20 Mar. 1930 **ED LOYCE**. No children.

537. **FRANK CHOWEN WINKLEY** [WILLIAM P. 244] He was born 3 Sep. 1864 at Fairbault, MN and died 28 Feb. 1956 at Minneapolis. He married 20 Feb. 1886 at Hudson, WI. **NORA MARY**, d/o **HENRY CLAY & LOUISE (HARMAN) ROBINSON**. She born 1871 and died 11 Dec. 1959. Occ. steam engineer. She accomplished writer, musician and composer. She wrote a newspaper column for a St. Paul paper. [All Our Yesterdays, Nora Winkley 1982]

Children: 1020. **DOROTHY**, b. 17 Apr. 1904.
           1021. **WILMA**, b. 9 Feb. 1889.
           1022. **AMY**, b. 24 Feb. 1899.
           1023. **HARRY FRANCIS**, b. 8 Jan. 1887, md. 9 Jan. 1909 **LILIAN V. COLEMAN**.

1024. **NORA (MARGIE)UERITE**, b. 8 July 1891.
1025. **HAZEL**, b. 17 Apr. 1896.
1026. **FRANK Jr. (Boy)**, b. 12 Dec. 1908.
1027. **WINIFRED**, b. 7 Oct. 1913.
1028. **LEA NORA**, b. 20 Jan. 1915.
1029. **GENEVIEVE**, b. 24 June 1916.
1030. **CHARLES**, b. 27 Sep. 1893, d. c1910.
1031. **WILLIAM**, b. 4 May 1902.

546. **MARK HENRY WINKLEY** [PAUL H. 252] He was born 23 May 1861 and died 21 April 1938. He married 23 May 1883 **FLORANCE ELLA TREFETHEN** d/o **EPHRAIM & PAMELIA TREFETHEN** at Strafford, NH. She born 1861 Eliot, Me. and died 1938. Res. Dover, NH. In 1870 census.

Children: 1050. **ERWIN/IRVING MARK/MARK ERVIN**, b. 13 Dec. 1885, md. 18 June 1911 **BESSIE MABEL ABBOTT**.
1051. **ALBERT MARK**, b. and d. 1889.

550. **PAUL HERMAN** or **HERMAN P. WINKLEY** [PAUL H. 256] He was born 1 Mar. 1874 and died 1961. He married 19 Aug. 1908 **WINIFRED E.** d/o **CHARLES & MARTHA (BODGE) CHESLEY** at Rochester. She born 17 Apr. 1870 and died 1920. [Delmar W. Goodman]

Children: 1060. **LEWIS C.**, b. 15 May 1905, d. 21 Feb. 1928 US Army. unmd.
1061. **HELEN**, b. 22 Aug. 1910, d. 23 Dec. 1989, unmd.
1062. **WILLIAM**, b. 3 Aug. 1916, d. 15 June 1974, unmd.

551. **CHARLES EUGENE WINKLEY** [PAUL H. 256] He was born 22 May 1873 and died 12 July 1956 at Plymouth, Mass. He married **HELEN RAYMOND**. She born 22 July 1886 and died 26 Oct. 1940. Res. Strafford, N.H.

Children: 1070. **CHARLES EUGENE Jr.**, b. 12 May
              1905, m.1, **AGNES RITA GOODWIN**
              1906-1960, m.2, 23 Aug. 1975
              EDITH JUDSON. Had: **DAVID** and
              LINDA A.
              1071. **VERA**, b. 4 Aug. 1908, unmd.
              1072. **CHARLOTTE**, b. 25 June 1915,
              md. **EDWARD STRESSEL.** 1 child.

EIGHTH GENERATION

1000. LEROY WINKLEY [JOSEPH A. 505] He was born c1869. He married at Strafford, NH 23 Dec. 1892 JENNIE B. GRAY. Occ. shoemaker. Res. Rochester, NH.

Children: 1200. CHARLES T., b. c1894, md. 7
June 1923 CORA P. GOODWIN d/o
AMAZIAH T. & BERTHA M. (GRANT)
GOODWIN. She b. 11 May 1895,
d. 6 Dec. 1923 at Rochester.
1201. ERNEST L., b. c1896, md. 5
Nov. 1919 MILDRED E. DAME d/o
J. HARRY & SARAH F. (VERITY)
DAME. She b. 1897.
1202. ETHEL MAY, b. 4 Jan. 1901, d.
26 Sep. 1904 at Rochester.

1003. FRANK B. WINKLEY (BENJ. F.) [JOSEPH A. 505] He was born 1877 and died 1951. He married 5 May 1904 BERTHA (HOWARD) HORNE, d/o ELBRIDGE W. & SARAH E. HOWARD. She born 1880 and died 1955.

Children: 1210. JOSEPH A., b. c1904, md. 28
Dec. 1931 DOROTHY COOK, etc.
1211.
1212.

1004. JEREMIAH S. WINKLEY [JOSEPH A. 505] He was born 10 Feb. 1879. He married 27 Mar. 1900 VIRA EMERSON, m.2, at Strafford, NH 27 Dec. 1901 LIZZIE E. GIBSON. She born 1880, d/o JAMES & EMMA GIBSON. She divorced him on grounds of cruelty on 27 Dec. 1901??, m.3, at Rochester, NH 23 Apr. 1906 SARAH F. LYNCH. She born 1872 d/o PATRICK & WINIFRED LYNCH. Children by 1st wife:

Children: 1215. HARRY A., b. c1901, md. 4 June
1923 EDDA R. POTVIN, d/o
ALPHONSO F. & ROSE (BROUELETTE)
POTVIN. She b. 1897.
1216. STEVE CLARK?

1023. **HARRY FRANCIS WINKLEY** [FRANK C. 537] He was born 8 Jan. 1887. He married 9 Jan. 1909 **LILLIAN VERONICA**, d/o **WILLIAM JAMES & BERTHA (HANSON) COLEMAN.** She born 12 July 1888 in Minn. Occ. electrician by trade. Prop. of Winkley grocery at Port Orchard, Wash.

Children: 1220. **ROBERT FRANCIS**, b. 14 Oct. 1909, md. 15 June 1936 **ELSE JANE TATE.**

1221. **NORA MARIAN**, twin, b. 3 Oct. 1911, unmd. Army nurse.

1222. **MARGARET SHIRLEY**, twin, b. 3 Oct. 1911, unmd.

1223. **CHARLES VINCENT**, b. 5 Oct. 1913, md. 1940 **MARCELLIA?**, Div. Vet WW2.

1224. **HARRY FRANCIS**, b. 20 June 1915, d. 14 Nov. 1937. unmd.

1225. **JANE ELIZABETH**, b. 14 Jan. 1923, md. 14 Jan. 1944 **LEWIS F. RICHARDSON.** 3 ch.

1226. **LILLIAN VERONICA ALICE**, b. 5 May 1926, md. 20 Feb. 1946 **CARL D. JESCH.** 6 ch. Author of Manuscript on Winkleys in 1966

1050. **ERWIN/IRVING MARK/MARK ERWIN WINKLEY** [MARK HENRY 545] He was born 13 Dec. 1885. He married 18 June 1911 **BESSIE MABEL ABBOTT**, d/o **GEORGE & JENNIE B. ABBOTT.** She b. c1893.

Children: 1230. **MARK ABBOTT**, b. Ossipee 22 May 1912, md. 18 Oct. 1936 **MARY TASKER SAWYER**, d/o **Wm L. & BERTHA (TASKER) SAWYER.**

1231. **MARGUWEITE RUTH ??**

PEDIGREE CHART:

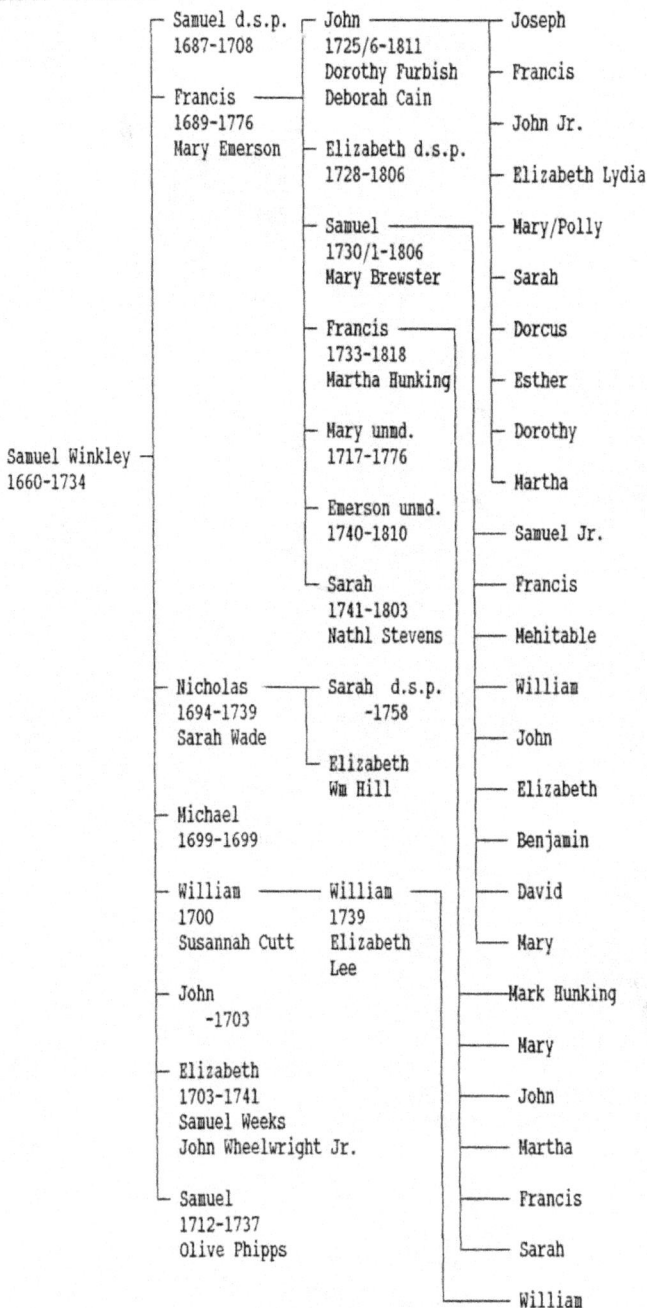

```
                              ┌ Samuel d.s.p. ┌ John ───────────── Joseph
                              │ 1687-1708     │ 1725/6-1811
                              │               │ Dorothy Furbish ┌ Francis
                              ├ Francis ──────┤ Deborah Cain
                              │ 1689-1776     │                 ├ John Jr.
                              │ Mary Emerson  ├ Elizabeth d.s.p.
                              │               │ 1728-1806       ├ Elizabeth Lydia
                              │               │
                              │               ├ Samuel ──────── Mary/Polly
                              │               │ 1730/1-1806
                              │               │ Mary Brewster   ├ Sarah
                              │               │
                              │               ├ Francis ─────── Dorcus
                              │               │ 1733-1818
                              │               │ Martha Hunking  ├ Esther
                              │               │
                              │               ├ Mary unmd. ──── Dorothy
    Samuel Winkley ──┐        │               │ 1717-1776
    1660-1734        │        │               │                 └ Martha
                     │        │               ├ Emerson unmd. ──── Samuel Jr.
                     │        │               │ 1740-1810
                     │        │               │                 ── Francis
                     │        │               └ Sarah
                     │        │                 1741-1803       ── Mehitable
                     │        │                 Nathl Stevens
                     │        ├ Nicholas ─────┬ Sarah d.s.p.   ── William
                     │        │ 1694-1739     │   -1758
                     │        │ Sarah Wade    │                ── John
                     │        │               └ Elizabeth
                     │        │                 Wm Hill        ── Elizabeth
                     │        ├ Michael
                     │        │ 1699-1699                      ── Benjamin
                     │        │
                     │        ├ William ────── William ─┐      ── David
                     │        │ 1700           1739      │
                     │        │ Susannah Cutt  Elizabeth │      └─ Mary
                     │        │                Lee       │
                     │        ├ John                     ├─Mark Hunking
                     │        │   -1703                  │
                     │        │                          ── Mary
                     │        ├ Elizabeth                │
                     │        │ 1703-1741                ── John
                     │        │ Samuel Weeks             │
                     │        │ John Wheelwright Jr.     ── Martha
                     │        │                          │
                     │        └ Samuel                   ── Francis
                     │          1712-1737                │
                     │          Olive Phipps             └─ Sarah
                     │
                     └──────────────────────────────────── William
```

UNKNOWN WINKLEY ENTRIES

A number of Winkley entries were found that could not be connected to the known families.

Benjamin Winkley, md. 10 Aug. 1835 Harmony Watson, Taunton, Me.
Catherine Winkley, In 1830 census at Providence, R.I.
Clarissa Winkley md. 30 Nov. 1830 Jones Plumer at Gilford, NH.
Cynthia G. Winkley, md. 25 Jan. 1893 James H. Currier, Strafford, NH
Daniel T. Winkley md. 15 Dec. 1847 Martha M. Mitchell at St. Louis, Mo.
David R. Winkley, md. 10 May 1842 Sarah J. Merrill, Newbury, MA.
Eliza Winkley 1815 - 1892, Pine Grove Cem. Barrington, NH.
Emaline L. (Clement) Winkley, d. 1835, Barrington, NH.
Emma H. Winkley, md. 12 Dec. 1842 Charles Hood, Taunton, Me.
George Winkley, 1830 census, Washington, DC.
George Winkley, Pittsfield, NH 5 July 1865 Guardianship. Had dau. Mary Frances
    and Emma, under age 14, to Dennis Winkley.
Hannah Winkley md. 30 July 1873 Benj. F. Trester Jr., Dearborn Co., Indiana.
Henry Winkley, 1800 census, Fairfield, Conn. [00001-00001]
Isaac Winkley 1790 census Providence, RI [1-0-3]
James Winkley 1830 census Monroe Co., NY.
James H. Winkley, d. 13 Sep. 1846, Greenland, NH.
John Winkley, md. 9 May 1802 Betty McGlothron Fryeburg, Me.
John Frank Winkley, md. 3 Feb. 1850 Abby C. Lefavour Manchester, NH.
Joseph Winkley 1789 tax roll Jefferson Co., KY.
Martha A. Winkley md. James H. Edgerly 1841 at Barrington, NH
Maria A. Winkley d. 13 Feb. 1895, 83-11, Portsmouth, NH.
Mary A. Winkley md. 6 Sep. 1846 Samuel V. Cole at Clyde, Mich.
Mehitable, d/o Sarah Winkley bp Apr. 1755, So. Church Portsmouth, NH.
Mehitable Winkley bp 27 July 1806, Lebanon, Me.
Mercy Winkley md. James White 1776 at Boston, Mass.
Nancy Winkley of Alton, NH md. 11 May 1815 Nathaniel Folsom.
Sally Winkley, md. 29 Nov. 1848 Francis Boardman, Salisbury, MA.
Sally w. Winkley md. 7 July 1831 Simon Straw of Strafford.
Samuel Winkley md. Mary Symmes at Portsmouth, NH.
Samuel Winkley, md. 31 Jan. 1825 Sally Swazey, Salisbury.
Sarah Winkley d. 9 Dec. 1871, 73-9, Sunnyside Cem. Barrington, NH.
Sarah Winkley d. 28 Aug. 1845, 69-5-20, Barrington, NH.
Secelia N., d/o James & Mary Ann Winkley, b. 10 Nov. 1848 Roxbury, MA.
Susanne Winkley md. James Barrick 1757 at Boston, Mass.
Thomas Winkley 1790 Census, Hallowell, Me. [2-3-4]

WIVES OF SAMUEL WINKLEY

THE WIVES OF SAMUEL WINKLEY

1ST WIFE:

A1. SARAH TRICKEY - Portsmouth, NH

She was the d/o **FRANCIS AND SARAH TRICKEY** [A2] of Kittery, Maine. She died before 14 May 1704. She married in 1684 **SAMUEL WINKLEY** at Portsmouth, NH.

> Children: i. SAMUEL, b. 28 Oct. 1687.
> ii. FRANCIS, b. c1689.
> iii. SARAH,
> iv. NICHOLAS, b. c1694.
> v. MICHAEL6, b. 13 May 1699.
> vi. WILLIAM, b. 5 Feb. 1700.
> vii. JOHN,
> viii. ELIZABETH, b. c1703.

A2. FRANCIS TRICKEY - Portsmouth, NH

Taxed Dover 1649, Portsmouth 1651 and owned 20 acres on Crooked Lane, Kittery, Maine in 1656. [Noyes] His land reached from Crooked Lane to Spruce Creek. [Me. Prov. & Court Rec., 4:158] Occupation fisherman. His Inv. taken 11 Apr. 1682, house and land. [Noyes] On subscription list 1658 at Portsmouth, NH [NHGR 1:9] His wife was named **SARAH**. Her estate granted 15 Apr. 1703 Crooked Lane property to Samuel Winkley who was the Admin. [Noyes] [Old Kittery & Her Families, Everett Stackpole, p. 19 (1903)]

> Children: i. SARAH, md. 1684 SAMUEL WINKLEY
> ii. JOHN, Inv. 17 May 1686 [York deeds V.]

COMMENTS:

No bapt. or md. was found in New England records or in England in the IGI. The name of TRICKEY is found primarily in Co. Devon, England for the 17th century.

SARAH TRICKEY Cont.

Sources:

Noyes, Sybil etal, Geneal. Dict. of Me. & NH,
   p. 693-4, Balt. (1972).
Pope, Chas., Pioneers of Me. & NH (1965),
   p. 204.
Tibbett, Chas. W., New Nampshire Geneal.
   Record, (1910) 1:9; 2:171, 235; 3:63.

WIVES OF SAMUEL WINKLEY Cont.;

2ND WIFE:

B1. HANNAH (CHECKLEY) ADAMS -

She was the d/o ANTHONY & HANNAH (WHEELWRIGHT) CHECKLEY [B2] and granddaughter of Rev. JOHN WHEELWRIGHT. She was born 19 Dec. 1674. She m.1, JOHN ADAMS. She m.2, 12 Dec. 1705 by Benjamin Wadsworth SAMUEL WINKLEY at Boston. She died by Feb. 1707/8. No children. [Boston Marriages 1700-1809]

B2. ANTHONY CHECKLEY - Boston

He was born c1636 the s/o JOHN CHECKLEY [B3]. He was 72 years old in 1708. He married HANNAH WHEELWRIGHT [B4]. She born 1644 at Boston, Mass. He m.2, LYDIA (SCOTTOW) GIBBS, widow of Capt. BENJAMIN GIBBS. She m.3, WILLIAM COLEMAN. Artillery Company 1664. Noted lawyer, attorney General, etc. No children by 2nd wife. [NEHGR 2:349] [N.E. Md prior to 1700, Torrey]

Children: i. JOHN, b. 30 Dec. 1664.
          ii. SARAH, b. 18 June 1668.
         iii. ELIZABETH, b. 8 May 1672, md.
              ___ LONG.
          iv. MARY, b. 14 Oct. 1673, md.
              _____ PERKINS.
          B1. HANNAH, b. 19 Dec. 1674, md.
              SAMUEL WINKLEY.

B3. JOHN CHECKLEY -

He was born 1609 and died 1 Jan. 1684/5 age 76 years. His first wife in unknown. He m.2, 5 May 1652 ANN d/o SIMON EYRES a surgeon.

Children: B2. ANTHONY, b. 1636, m.1, HANNAH
              WHEELWRIGHT, m.2, LYDIA (SCOTTOW)
              GIBBS.
          ii. JOHN, b. 21 Apr. 1653.
         iii. ANN, b. 22 Apr. 1659, d. 20 June
              1661.

WIVES OF SAMUEL WINKLEY Cont.

iv. **SAMUEL**, b. 26 Nov. 1661, d. 1712.
v. **ANN**, b. 4 Aug. 1669.

REMARKS:

The name of CHECKLEY is found in records of the city of London. Sir Robert was Sheriff of London 1400-2 and Lord Mayor 1411 and 1421. Sir Robert died in 1422. His brother William was Sheriff of London 1408-9 and 1411. Their brother Henry was the eldest son of Thomas Checkley of Higham Ferrers, Co. Northamptonshire. Henry was born 1362 and died April 1443. He founded All Souls college at Oxford. Relationship to the Checkley immigrants is unknown. [NEHGR 2:234]

B4. **HANNAH WHEELWRIGHT** - Boston

She was the daughter of **Rev. JOHN & MARIE (STORRE) WHEELWRIGHT [B5]**. She was born about 1644. She married **ANTHONY CHECKLEY [B2]**.

B5. **Rev. JOHN WHEELWRIGHT** - Lincolnshire

He was born about 1594 possibly at Bilsby, Co. Lincolnshire, England. He was the son of **ROBERT WHEELWRIGHT**. He died 15 Nov. 1679 at Salisbury, Mass. He married first 8 Nov. 1621 **MARIE** the daughter of **Rev. THOMAS STORRE [B7]** of Bilsby, Co. Lincolnshire. She possibly born 12 Nov. 1604 at St. Benedict, Lincoln. She died 18 May 1629 at Bilsby, England. He married second **MARY** daughter of **EDWARD HUTCHINSON**. He graduated Sydney College at Cambridge BA in 1614 and AM in 1618. He was a minister at Bilsby in Co. Lincolnshire. He is named in Inquest Post Mortem of cousin Robert Wheelwright 29 Aug. 1622. His age was 27 years. [IPM Chancery Series 2, v.765, #42] [NEHGR 68:74]

WIVES OF SAMUEL WINKLEY Cont.

He came to Boston 26 May 1636. Removed to Exeter 1638. He was the first minister and founder of Exeter, NH. At Wells 1642 then Hampton, NH in 1647 where he was the 3rd minister. He returned to England in 1657, but later came back in 1662 to Salisbury, Mass. Children bapt. at Bilsby. [Savage][Dow]

Children: i. **JOHN**, bp 6 Oct. 1622. (did not emigrate)
      ii. **WILLIAM**, bp 10 Feb. 1626/7 at Alfred, bur. 19 May 1627.
    iii. **SUSANNA**, bp 22 May 1628, md. **EDWARD RICHWORTH Jr.**

by 2nd Wife:
     iv. **KATHERINE**, bp 4 Nov. 1630, m.1, **ROBERT NANNEY**, m.2, **EDWARD NAYLOR**.
      v. **MARIE**, bp 19 May 1632 at Alfred, d. 28 July 1632.
     vi. **SAMUEL**, b. 1635, md. **ESTHER HOUCHIN**. Had: **JOHN, JOSEPH MARY** and **HANNAH**.
    vii. **MARY**, bp. 25 June 1637 at Boston, m.1, 4 Dec. 1660 **EDWARD LLOYD**. m.2, 2 Oct. 1667 **THEODORE ATKINSON**.
   viii. **ELIZABETH**, md. **GEORGE PERSON**.
     ix. **REBECCA**, md. 4 Dec. 1660 **SAMUEL MAVERICK**, m.2, 12 Jan. 1672 **WILLIAM BRADBURY**.
    B4. **HANNAH**, md. 1671 **ANTHONY CHECKLEY**.
     xi. **SARAH**, md. **RICHARD CRISPE**.

B6. ROBERT WHEELWRIGHT - Lincolnshire

Yeoman of Cumberworth and Saleby, Co. Lincolnshire. He was buried at Saleby 23 Feb. 1612/3. He married in 1591 **KATHERINE (MAWER) KINGERLY** at Wainfleet, Lincolnshire. She died 8 July 1605 at Salesby. She was the perhaps the daughter of **WILLIAM MAWER [B8]** bp. 18 May 1573 at Covenham, Linc. She was born 1560. She m.1, 2 Apr. 1581 **RICHARD KINGERLY**. He died c1591.

WIVES OF SAMUEL WINKLEY Cont.;

They had two sons Robert and Thomas. [NEHGR
21:363-5, 74:51] His will 13 Oct. 1611 proved 7
Mar. 1612/3. Names wife Katherine, daughters and
son John. Consist. Court Lincoln 1612, fo. 638,
[NEHGR 68:74].

Children: B5. **JOHN**, b. c1594, md 8 Nov. 1621
               MARIE STORRE..
           ii. **ELIZABTH**, bp. 24 June 1596.
           iii. **KATHERINE**, bp. 23 Mar.
               1599/1600.
           ov. **ELLEN/ELYNOR**, bp. 29 June 1601.

B7. **THOMAS STORRE** Bilsby, Co. Lincolnshire

He was the vicar at Bilsby. He died 26 March
1623. [NEHGR 21:364]

Children: B5. **MARIE**, b. 12 Nov. 1604, d. 18
               May 1629, md. 8 Nov. 1621 **JOHN**
               WHEELWRIGHT.
           ii. **AUGUSTINE**, md. **SUSANNA**
               HUTCHINSON.

B8. **THOMAS MAWER** - Willoughby, Co. Lincolnshire

His will proved 1597, Consist. court Lincoln. He
married 1st 17 Aug. 1557 **JOAN LEMING** and married
2nd 3 Aug. 1560 **MARGARET MASON** at Willoughby.
Which wife was the mother of daughter Katherine
is unknown. [NEHGR 74:52]

Children: B6. **KATHERINE**, bp 18 May 1573, md.
               ROBERT WHEELWRIGHT.

Sources Checkley:

  Whittemore, Henry, Geneal. Guide to the Early
    Settlers of Amer. (1967)
  Torrey, Clarence A., New England Marriages
    Prior to 1700, p.148 (1983).
  NEHGR 2:349, 61:66.

WIVES OF SAMUEL WINKLEY Cont.

Sources Wheelwright:

Dow, Joseph, Hist. of the Town of Hampton, NH,
  p. 1039, (1893)
Heard, John Jr., John Wheelwright 1592-1679,
  Boston (1930)
NEHGR 68:75, 74:31.
Cushing, Gertrude W., Geneal. of the Wells
  Family, Milw. (1903).
Savage, James A., Geneal. Dist. of the First
  Settlers of New England, Boston (1860)
Merrill, Nancy C., Exeter, NH 1888-1988,
NEHGR: 1:150-1; 21:315, 363-6; 22:83; 68:51-3,
  73-7; 74:51.

WIVES OF SAMUEL WINKLEY Cont.

3RD WIFE:

C1. ELIZABETH (HUNKING) FERNOLD

She was the d/o JOHN & ANN (HUNKING) HUNKING of
Star Island, Isles of Shoal. She died 6 Oct.
1723 and is buried at Point of Graves Cemetery,
Portsmouth, NH. [NH Gen. Rec. 1:19] She m.1,
THOMAS FERNOLD. He born 1668 and died 1709? She
m.2, in Nov. 1712 SAMUEL WINKLEY in Portsmouth,
NH. [NHGR 5:41]

> Child: i. SAMUEL, bp 12 Nov. 1721, d.
>   1737, md. OLIVE PHIPPS.

C2. JOHN HUNKING - Portsmouth/Star Is.

Fisherman on Isles of Shoals 1650. He married
about 1651 ANN d/o HERCULES HUNKING [C3] of Star
Island. Family relationship unknown. She was 42
in 1671/2. He had land grant 13 Jan. 1666 of 8
acres "below Boiling Rock" at Portsmouth. At
Portsmouth, NH in 1650. Trial 2 Aug. 1674 [NH
Court Files 3:85] Served on Petit Jury 22 Oct.
1677 [NH Prov. Papers 17:524] He was the master
of ENDEAVER and owner in other vessels in 1681.
[NH Prov. Papers 19:667] Com. Ensign in 1680.
Called Sergt. in 1681. His will dated 25 Aug.
1681 was proved 7 June 1682. He names his wife
as RICHORD. She m.2, GEORGE SNELL, resided in
Boston. In her will dated 24 Sep. 1691, proved
23 Apr. 1695 she gave £10 to her step daughter
ELIZABETH HUNKING. All children by 1st wife.
[Noyes]

> Children: i. JOHN, b. 2 Mar. 1651/2, d. in
>   England July 1666.
>   ii. HERCULES, b. 11 July 1656. Not
>   named in will.
>   iii. JOHN, b. 6 Apr. 1660, d. by 10
>   May 1725, md. 23 Sep. 1682 MARY
>   LEIGHTON.
>   iv. PETER, b. 20 Mar. 1662/3.
>   v. AGNES, b. 2 June 1665.

WIVES OF SAMUEL WINKLEY Cont.

       vi. **WILLIAM**, 6 Jan. 1667/8, D. 1754,
          md. 12 May 1692 **SARAH PARTRIDGE**.
      vii. **MARK**, b. 17 May 1670, md.
          29 June 1697 **MARY HARVEY**.
          She m.2, 5 Dec. 1699 Rev.
          JOHN NEWMARCH.
(C1) viii. **ELIZABETH**, d. 6 Oct. 1723, m.1,
          THOMAS FERNOLD, m.2, Nov. 1712
          SAMUEL WINKLEY.

C3. HERCULES HUNKING Star Is./Portsmouth, NH

He was bp 13 June 1604 s/o **HERUCLES HUNKING** of
St. Stephen by Saltesh, Co. Cornwall, England.
He was a fishing master on Star Is. by 1649. He
removed to Portsmouth, NH. Granted 50 acre in
1652. Selectman 1658. Subscribed to support of
Minister 14 Feb. 1658/9. [NHGR 1:9] His will
dated 21 Aug. 1659. Inventory taken 6 Sep. 1659.
Had 3 boats and a house and a stage on Star
Island. Widow **BEATON HUNKING**, 8 Nov. 1659 [Essex
Court Rec.] She m.2, **WILLIAM HEARL**.

Children: C1. **ANN/AGNES**, b. c1630, md. **JOHN
            HUNKING** C2.
       ii. **MARK**, Portsmouth, NH 1666 - 1690

C4. HERCULES HUNKING Cornwall, England

He was born c1580 the s/o **ROGER HUNKING** of St
Stephen by Saltesh, Co. Cornwall, England.

Children: C3. **HERCULES**, bp 13 June 1604,
       ii. **MARK/MARCUS**, bp 25 June 1615.
      iii. **WILLIAM**, md. 12 May 1692 **SARAH
           PARTRIDGE**, d/o JOHN.?

C5. ROGER HUNKING Resided at Saltesh, Cornwall,
England.

Children: C4. **HERCULES**, b. c1580.

WIVES OF SAMUEL WINKLEY Cont.

Sources:

Noyes, Sybil etal, Geneal. Dict. of Me & NH,
  p. 359-360, Balt. (1972).
Pope, Chas. H., Pioneers of Me. & NH (1973)
Whittemore, Henry, Guide to the Early Settlers
  of Amer. (1967)
Tibbetts, Chas. W., New Hampshire Geneal.
  Record, Dover (1910) 1:9, 75, 99; 2:25, 235;
  3:50, 104.

PEDIGREE CHART: WIVES OF SAMUEL WINKLEY

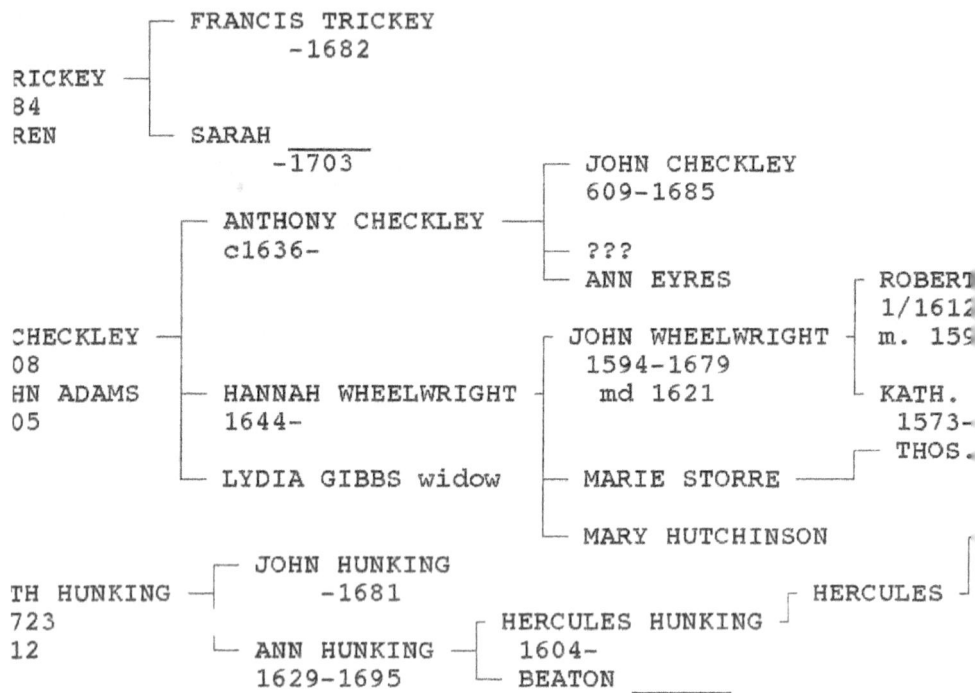

```
                ┌─ FRANCIS TRICKEY
                │       -1682
  RICKEY  ──────┤
  84            │
  REN           └─ SARAH _____
                        -1703
                                      ┌─ JOHN CHECKLEY
                                      │     609-1685
                ┌─ ANTHONY CHECKLEY ──┤
                │     c1636-          ├─ ???
                │                     └─ ANN EYRES              ┌─ ROBERT
                │                                               │   1/1612
  CHECKLEY ─────┤                     ┌─ JOHN WHEELWRIGHT ──────┤   m. 159
  08            │                     │     1594-1679           │
  HN ADAMS      ├─ HANNAH WHEELWRIGHT ┤       md 1621           └─ KATH.
  05            │     1644-           │                             1573-
                │                     │                         ┌─ THOS.
                └─ LYDIA GIBBS widow  ├─ MARIE STORRE ──────────┘
                                      │
                                      └─ MARY HUTCHINSON

                ┌─ JOHN HUNKING
                │     -1681                                  ┌─ HERCULES ┘
  TH HUNKING ───┤                     ┌─ HERCULES HUNKING ───┘
  723           │                     │   1604-
  12            └─ ANN HUNKING ───────┤
                     1629-1695        └─ BEATON _____
```

APPENDIX

WILL OF SAMUEL WINKLEY

In the name of God Amen the thirteenth day of Novem. Anno Domini 1726. I Sam[l]
Winkley of Portsm.; in New Hampshire in New England Esq. being sick and weak in
body But of perfect mind & memory and Knowing the mortality of my Body, and y[t],
it is appointed for all men once to Dye do make and ordain this my Last will and
Testament. That is to say principally and first of all I Give and Recommend my
Soul to God that gave it and my Body. I Recommend to the earth to be buried in
christain and Decent manner nothing doubting but att the General Resurection I
shall receive the same again by the Allmighty power of God. And as touching such
worldly Estate wherewith it hath pleased God to Bless me in this life I Give,
Demise, & Dispose of the Same in the following manner and form. - - - - - - -

Item, I will y[t] my just Debts and funerall charges be paid out of my Estate by
my Executors hereafter named.

Item, I Give and Demise unto my son Francies Winkley all that Dwelling house and
land att Crocked Lane in Kittery where he liv,d and I formerly liv,d my self with
all the priveledg[s]: and appurtinancies thereunto Belonging or in way
apperti=aining, to have and to hold to him my said son Francies Winkley and the
heirs of his Body Lawfully Begotten but if he Dyes without issue of his Body
Lawfully Begotten then I will and Bequeath the same to be equally Divided amongst
my other children or theire Representatives. I having given my said son Francies
other things out of my Estate for his preserment allready and have made all his
Breatheren and Sisters to Quit clame any Interest in Said Estate to my Said son
Francies Winkley.

Item, I Give and Bequeath unto my son Nich[o] Winkley, besides what money I have
allready given him all[t]y. My Rights in the New Town of Barrington and whatsoever
Estate I may be entitled to there as I am an Inhabitant of the Town of Portsm.
aforesaid to be to him his heirs and assigns for ever allso I give him my bed I
lye on and Boulster and two pillows and Blanketts and one Blew Rugg and Beadstead
and my bible y[t] was my fathers and wh[t] plate I Design,d for him I have given him
allready.

Item, I give and bequeath unto my son Wm Winkley all y[t] hundred acres of Land in
the Town of Berwick in the County of York in New England wich was granted me by
the Town of Kittery. To have and to hold to him my said son William his heirs and
assigns forever. Allso I give unto him a silver; porrenger made by Mr. Buminer
& six silver spoons with mine and his mothers name on them and silver whistle and
two silver Canns wth my name on them & made by Mr. Tyler and my Bed in my Kitchen
chamber Blanketts & Boulster the other Blew Rugg and Bedstead. Allso I give unto
my said Son Wm two large silver porrengers and one silver cann mark,d S -W and
the Goldsmiths Mark in each ER - - - - - -

Item, I Give unto my Daughter Eliz^a: Weeks besides what I have allready given her, six cain chairs and couch y^t I bought of Capt. Paxton & seven pewter Dishes twelve plates a quilt and Blanketts & allso if so happen y^t she should be a widow and desire itt, I give unto her during her widowhood the use of my corner shop on the place where I now live & the yard before it and my new cellar under my house and about a third part of the garden, if she see good to make use of itt. All this to be without paying any Rent for the same. The pewter Dishes my daughter Elizabeth have them already sent her.

Item, I give unto my son Saml Winkley all my now Dwelling house and land in Portsm^o aforesaid with all the house priveledges and appurtentenancies to the same Belonging in any way appertenancies to have and to hold to him my said son Saml Winkley and the heirs of his Body lawfully Begotten, allways Excepting the use and improvements of what I have before given my Daughter Elizabeth during her widowhood if itt si happens, but if my said Samuel should Die without issue of his body lawfully Begotten then my will is y^t the said house and Land be equally Divided Between the rest of my children or their Representatives. I allso give unto my son Sam. the sum of one hundred and twenty fice pounds current paper Bills of credit, to be put at Interest on good Security for the Bringing up my said son and also a feather Bed my Camblett curtains Blanketts White Rugg Bedstead Curting Rods Boulster and pillows and he to have his mothers Bed and all the furniture Belonging to it and my Silver Tankard made by Mr. Greenough and six Silver spoons made by Mr. Cunny and seven Silver spoons marked with his mothers former name and a silver cup I Bo^t of Capt. John Hunkings and a little two Lard silver cup and silver Botkin and a silver porrenger; y^t is at his Sister Week's in Boston and five Gold Rings one of them a Seal Ring with my name onit two molders of Gold and one small purse Gold about Six shillings Value and the twelve cain chairs in the Kitchen Chamber and four pewter Dishes and six pewter plates. If my son Saml should Dye before marrriage or before he comes to age without issue of his body Lawfully Begotten then all the above Bequests after his funerall charges and Lawfull Debts are paid the Remainder to be equally Divided amongest my other children or their Representatives. - - - - - -

Item, I Give unto my Kin woman Elizth Hunking y^t now lives with me Ten pounds in money or out of my goods to be paid her by my Executors and one Silver spoon made by Dan$_l$ Greenough.

Item, Whatever is left of my Estate after Gifts and legacies above Exprest and my funerall charges; paid my will it that it shall be equally divided; amongest my children and their Representatives; - my Duaghter Sarah Langdon to have her part, of that her name not being mentioned before in this will, I having paid her: her portion allready. - - - - -

Item, I give unto Mary Grant my old Servt a silver spoon made by Dan. Greenough. - - - - -

And do hereby Desire my Trusty & well Beloved friends Geo; Jaffrey Esqr and Mr. Ephraim Dennett both of Portsm^o: aforesaid to accept and to be the Executors of this my last Will and Testam^t and Guardian to my son Samuel until he come to age - and I do by these presents constitute and appoint them the said Geo^e: Jaffrey and Ephraim Dennett Executors of this my Last Will and Testament: and Guradian to my Said son Samuel Winkley untill he come to age and I do hereby Revoak Disanull & Disallow all former and other wills and testaments by me made. Allowing & holding form and Vallied this and no other to be my Last Will and Testament. In Witness; whereof I have hereunto Set my hand and Seal the day and year first above mentioned.

Signed Seal'd Deliver'd
Declared & pronounced
by me the Said Samuel
Winkley to be my last
Will & Testament in presence of

the Word (one) in Saml bequest
mended before Sealing

Samuel Winkley

/Samuel Shackford
        the
John   Shackford
    mark of
Saml Jelfrey

Prov^e: of New   The sixth day of May Anno Domini 1736 then the Exec^rs to
Hampshire   the foregoing will presenting the same to be proved Sam
                       Jelfrey & John Shachford two of the Witnesses personally
                            appeared before Benj. Gambling Esqr Judge of the probate of
Wills for said Prov^e and made Solemn oath that they were present and saw the said Samuel Winkley Deceased sign seal & Declare the same to be last will and testament and that at the Doing thereof he was of a sound disposing mind and memory and allso that the with . . . . .

Source: NH Prov. Probate Will #930.

LETTER OF ADMINISTRATION

Province of   By the Honble Benj^a Gambling Esq & Judge of the Probate of Wills
New Hamp.   and for Granting letters of Administration on the Estate of
                    persons deceased having goods chattels Rights or Credits in the
Province aforesaid - To all unto whom these Present shall come Greeting. Know
ye that upon the day of the date hereof before me in Portsmouth in the Province
afores: the will of Samuel Winkley late of Portsmouth afors^d Esqr Deceased to
these presents annexed was Proved approved and allowed who having while he lived
and at the time of his Death Goods Chattels Rights or Credits in the Province
afors^d And the Probate of the said will and Power of Committing ____: of all &
singular the Goods Chattels Rights and Credits of the said deceased and his Will
in any manner concerning is hereby Committed unto George Jaffrey & Ephraim Dennet
both of Porstmouth aforesaid Esqr. same will named well & faithfully to Exec^c in
the Execute the said will and to administer the Estate of the Said Deceased
according there unto and to make a true & perfect Inventory of All and singular
the Goods chattels, rights and Credits of the Said Deceased and to Exhibit the
same Into the Registry of the Court of Probate for the Province aforesaid at or
before the Last Wednesday of August next ensuring and also to tender a plain &
true accompt of their Said Admin^r upon oath.

In testimony whereof I have hereunto Set my hand & the Seal of the Said Court
of Probate at Portsm afored^d the Sixth day of May Anno domini 1736.

                                        Benj^a Gambling
William Parker, Reg.

Source: V14, p.285 NH Probate Records.

february, 21 1662

In the nam of god, amon; I, Richard Seaward being
weeake of body, yett in sound, and parfitt memmory
doe ordaine this to bee my last will and testiment
Item I giue twoe pound to my grandchild John
Jackson; Item the next point I giue Richard Jackson
Item the wole point to Mary Seawards; Item the rest
of the lands equally to be deuided betweext Richards Sea
wards; and Richards Jackson; Item my houshold goods equally
to be diuided betweext Richard Seawards; and Richards Jack
son; Item my hole parte of the biskoll and pecayo equity
to be diuided betwext Richard Seawards children and
Richard Jacksons children; Item fowtene pound of mony
which my brother Roggor Seawards is in deforts to mee I
giue to my sonn Richard Seaward; my detos binge
full payed; I doe heere apoint the saieds Richard Sea
wards and Richards Jackson my ouer seeors wittnes
my hand and seale this yeare and day, aboue written

for the lands which my brother Roggor doth liue in hee is
quietly to injoy it for his life time; with out any
mulligation

wittnes   Richard
  Nichlos winkley   Seaward   his marke
  Thomas Branfeld
  Tho: Besson
  Will: Attword

Nichlas winkley & the Branfell came
before mee & made oath that this will
was the act & deed of Richard sawerd
semen a little before his death —
  before mee Brian Pendleton
                Comisioner
this will being brought into Court held at douer 1 July 1663
the Court finding it to perfect for want of depudies
doe therfore apoynt Richard Seward & Richard
Jackson administrators
              Roter of Court Elias Stileman Coppie

WILL OF RICHARD SEWARD, 21 Feb. 1662/3:

In the name of god amen, I Richard Seaward being weeke of body yett in sound and perfitt memory dow ordaine this to bee my last will and testament. Item I give drake point to my grane Child John Jackson, Item the next point I give Richard Jackson, Item the rocke point to Mary Seaward, Item the rest of the lands equally to be divied betwext Richard Seaward, and Richard Jackson, Item my housells goods equally to be divied betwxt Richard Seaward and Richard Jackson, Item my hole parte of the visell and cargo equally to be divied betwext Richard Seaward children and Richard Jackson children, Item fortene pound of mony which my brother Rogger Seaward is indeted to me I give to my sonn Richard Seaward, my detes binge first payed, I doe heare apoint the said Richard Seaward and Richard Jackson my over seeres, witnes my hand and seale the yeare and day aboufe ritten. For the land which my brother Rogger doth live in hee is quietly to injoy if for his life time: with out any mullisation.

witnes Nicklous Winkleey   Richard
        Thomas Branfell   Seaward his mark
        Tho: Besson
        Will Atwood

Nikolas Winklye & Tho Branfell came before mee & made oath that this will was the akt & deed of Richard Saword Senier - a little before his death --

                        Before me Brian Pendleton
                        Commisioner

This will being brought into Court held at Dover 1st July 1663 & the Court finding it Imperfict for want of executors doe therefore appoynt Richard Seward & Richard Jackson Administrator.

                    By ord^r of court Elias Stilman clerk

WILL OF RICHARD SEAWARD   PORTSMOUTH

In the name of God Amen. I Richard Seaward of Portsmouth in Piscataque River in New england being sick & weake in body but p'fect in mind & memory doe make & appaynt this to be my last will & testament as followeth ____.

Imps. My will is that the land belonging to me and Richard Jackson on the ragged rock be equally divided between us and that part wch is to be my share I give and bequeath to my wife Mary Seaward and my children to be equally divided amongst them _ The dividend betweene me & the said Rich Jackson to begin at a great elme stump at the head of a branch & from thence to Rich Jacksons fence on the top of a hill and soe into the woods to one bounded tree lyinge northeasterlie.

It. My will is that the twenty six acres of land adjoyninge to the former ____ the land was layd out by men appoynted by the towne be alsoe equally divided betweene my said wife & children.

It. My will is that thirteene acres of land wch lyes to the norward of the rugged rock wch is betweene Richard Jackson & myself and bought by us both of roger Knight to be divided betweene us and that halfe wch falls to my share my will is that it be likewise divided betweene my wife & children. But if richard Jackson doe make sale of it then the one halfe of the produce wch falls to my share to be divided as afore said betweene my wife and children.

It. My will is that Knight Island be likewise equally divided betweene me & richard Jackson - and the helfe that falls to my share to be equally divided betweene my wife & children - And my will is that there be noe sale made of w^{t} my part is in the said Island on noe acct whatever.

It. My will is that w^{t} tobacco I have in the vessell called the Prosporouse and like. Will what is due to me from Mr. Richard Cutt & Mr. Fryer to me wth the tobacco due to me in the province of Maryland to be sold for the sattisfying of my debts and what is above that wch will sattisfie my said debts to be put to use for the maintenance of my wife & children. And for the rest of my estate in w^{t}nature kind or quallatie _____ it be I give & bequeath to my wife & children to be equally divided betweene them. And I doe hereby appoynt my lovring friends Major Nicholas shapley & Mr. Nathl Fryer to be the overseers of this my will untill my children be of age.

In witness whereof I have & hereunto set my hand this 1st day of August 1667.

Richard Seaward

Testes.

Testt by me Thomas Miller
Arthur Rope

REVOLUTIONARY WAR SERVICE

1. **EMERSON WINKLEY**, [16] Kittery, Me. militia [Soldiers, Sailors & Patriots of the Rev. War, Me., Carlton E. Fisher (1983)]

2. **JOHN WINKLEY**, [11] Kittery, Me. Enlisted 5 Nov. 1775 Capt. Wm Deering Co. of Carpenters. Nov. 1775 at Fort Sullivan. On alarm list 23 June and 20 Oct. 1785. [NH State Papers, v.18, p.240]

3. **JOSEPH WINKLEY**, [?] NH service. Enlisted 1 July 1780 for 6 months, 1st Regt Cont. Army, age 23, 5' 7". dark complexion [NH State Papers, v.16, p. 60][Index to Rev. War Service Records, Virgil D. White, (1995)]

4. **SAMUEL WINKLEY**, [41] NH. Capt. McDuffee's co. Enlisted 8 Sep. 177, deserted Oct. 19th, Marched to Bennington, Vt. Wages 6s 9d. [NH State Papers, v.15, p. 299]

5. **SAMUEL WINKLEY Jr.**, [?] NH. Served Pvt. in Evan's Regt. of NH Militia. [   ]

[   ] Ancestor Number

DOVER E

PUBLISHED EVERY THURSDAY MORNING, BY GEORGE WADLEI(

THURSDAY MORNING, M

Miscellany.

HISTORICAL MEMORANDA.
Number 221.

Winkley Family.

Francis Winkley(1) son of Samuel (1) lived at Crooked Lane in Kittery, Me. His occupation was that of boatbuilder having learned his trade in Boston, Mass. He mar. Mary dau. of Rev. John Emerson of Portsmouth, N. H. She died 17 March 1745, aged 41. Their children were John(1) b. 1726, d. 31 Mar. 1811, aged 85, Elizabeth b. 1728 d. at Barrington, 23 Nov. 1806, aged 78. Samuel (3) b. 9 Mar. 1731, d. 29 Nov. 1806. Francis(2) b. 1733, d. 9 Oct. 1818. Mary b. 1736. d. at Boston, Mass.,1 Dec., 1776. Emerson b. 1738, d. at Barrington, 17 Sept., 1810. Sarah b. 1740 d. 6 Feb. 1803. The daus. were not married.

John Winkley(1) son of Francis (1) mar. Deborah Caln of Kittery where they lived. She d. 27 Mar. 1829 aged 95. They had chil., Joseph, Francis(3), John(2), Elizabeth, Mary, Sarah, Dorcas, Esther, Dorathy and Martha. Joseph died a young man. Francis(3) mar. Martha Brown of Kittery. They lived in Ports. He died at sea. They had children, John(3), William (4) and Martha M., who mar. Seth Leighton of Dover. John(2) the Clockmaker mar. Lydia Hall of Newington. He died 18 May 1813, aged 46. They had chil., James who mar. Martha Hicks. He died 13 Sept. 1846, aged 50. He left no chil. Lydia wife of John(2) and two dau. died with the Shakers at Canterbury N. H. The dau. were Charlotte and Clarissa.— Elizabeth dau. of John(1) mar. Mr. Boosby of Limerick, Me. Mary mar. Mr. Stone also of L.— Sarah mar. Wm. Tibbetts of Brookfield N. H.— Dorcas mar Mr. Wiggin also of B. Esther mar. Joseph Bouson of Kittery. Dorathy mar. a Mr. Blaney of Ports. Martha mar a Mr. Cutton also of P.

Samuel Winkley(3) son of Francis(1) was a joiner by trade, having served his time with Mark Langdon of Ports. He mar. Mary dau. of Samuel Brewster of P. She was b. 13 April 1734,d. 3 Nov. 1816, aged 82. Her mother was Margaret Waterhouse grand dau. of Richard Waterhouse who owned and occupied Pierce Island at Ports. in 1688. Samuel(3) lived and died in Barrington.— Their chil. were Samuel(4) b. 24 Dec. 1756, d. 18 May 1812. Francis(4), the Shaker Elder, b. 28 Mar. 1759, d. 20 June 1847. Mehitable b. 10 May 1761, d. 22 Sept. 1824. William(2) b. 31 Aug.1763,d.29 July 1845.Dea.John(3) b. 17 Nov. 1776, d. 8 Jan. 1843. Elizabeth b. 9 Mar. 1769, d. 29 July 1850. Benjamin b. 3 Jan. 1772, d. 30 Sept. 1851. Col. David b. 4 July 1775, d. 18 Dec. 1852. Mary b. 3 Aug. 1777.

Samuel Winkley(4),son of Samuel(3) mar Olive Kingman of Barrington, where they lived. She died 17 Oct. 1822, aged 71. Their children were Elizabeth, who mar. Jona. Drew of Durham,— They lived in Barrington. Mary mar. Richard Furber of Farmington. Mehitable mar. Pierce P. Farber also of F. Olive not mar. Samuel(5) died a young man not mar. Abiah mar. Augustus Rollins, Esq.; of Rollinsford.

Francis Winkley(4),son of Samuel (3), mar. Sarah Libby of Dover. They had chil. Samuel(6) and Enoch. Francis(4) and wife joined the Shakers at Canterbury where he became a ruling Elder. Their sons left the Shakers and settled in Amesbury, Mass. Samuel(6) mar., but left no chil. Enoch mar. Mary Locke of Seabrook, chil. were John F., Francis J., Mary S. and Sarah L.

Mehitable Winkley, dau. of Samuel(3), mar. Paul Tasker of Barnstead. They left no children.

William(2) son of Samuel(3) mar. 1st Martha Clark of Barrington. She was b. 25 Feb. 1763, d. 11 Oct. 1780. They had one son, Paul. 2d wife Mary, dau. of Francis Winkley(2). 3d wife Tamson dau. of Dea. Benjamin Pierce of Dover. She was b. 6 June 1780, d. 28 Jan. 1858. Paul, son of William(2) b. 5 Oct 1780, d. 28 Nov. 1820. He mar. Abigail, dau. of Moses Rollins of Loudon. Their chil. were Paul T. who mar. Abigail, dau. of Hon. Job Otis of Strafford. They live in Newbury, Mass., chil. Abbie A., Sarah M., Job O., Mary G., Viola F. and Paul T. Martha M. dau. of Paul died young. William M. died not mar. Benjamin F. mar. Cyntha Kimball. They live in Strafford. Abigail A. mar. Charles Clyde of Derry, chil. Martha J., Maria A., Charles M. and Benjamin F. David and Holman sons of Paul died young.

William(2) chil. by 2d wife were William(3) b. 23 Jan. 1789., Martha b. 3 Jan. 1791, d. 11 Nov. 1818, Mary b. 27 July 1793, Ann b. 27 Jan. 1796, Sarah b. 22 Feb. 1798, Henry b. 9 Nov. 1803, Samuel b. 5 Oct. 1805, Joanna b. 13 Dec 1810.

William(3) mar. Sarah dau. of Richard Hussey, she died 10 Jan. 1862, aged 67. They had dau. Martha A. b. 9 Nov. 1819. She mar. Jeremiah Waterhouse, Jr. They have one son b. 31 Jan. 1845. Mary mar. Joseph Hussey. He d. 23 Nov. 1853. They had no chil. Ann mar. Jeremiah Buzzell. He died 2 July 1853, aged 62. They had chil., Martha W. mar. Dr. William Waterhouse, John J. mar. Sarah Tuttle. He d. 26 June 1857, aged about 31. Mary b. 12 Nov. 1825, Wm. H. b. 23 June 1820, Mark F. b. 26 Nov. 1831, d. 1835, Charles F. b. 20 Feb. 1837. Sarah dau. of William(2) lives with her sister Buzzell at the old homestead. Henry, son of Wm. (2) is a wholesale merchant in the city of New York not mar. Samuel(9) youngest son of Wm. (2) lives in Barrington. His 1st wife was Nancy Foss of Strafford, 2d wife Lydia Foye of Dover, chil. Mary E. b. 13 Oct. 1840, Abbie V. b. 18 Nov. 1844. His first wife b. 13 May 1808 d. 20 March 1836. Joanna youngest dau. of Wm(2) mar. Watson Hayes, Esq., of Rochester, chil. were William W. b. 24 May 1830, George L. b. 5 Dec 1831, d. 23 July 1854, Mary J. b. 24 June 1834, Albert W. b. 27 Nov. 1836, Anguline b. 26 Mar. 1839, Orvil H. b. 4 June 1844, Norman P. b. 9 July 1849.

Dea. John Winkley son of Samuel(3) mar. Mary Swain. They lived and died in Strafford. She d. 4 Feb. 1854, aged 90. Their chil. were Daniel, who mar. Sarah dau. of Hon. Job Otis. They had chil. Otis and Daniel Swain. Elder John, son of Dea. John, mar. Susan dau. of Stephen Otis of S. They had one son Jeremiah who mar. Elizabeth Hill of S. Samuel(7) mar. Nancy Fifield.— They lived in Plainfield N. H. Their chil. were Alonzo and Mary A. Swain lived in Boston. He mar. 1st Harriet Hammond, chil. were Mary A. and Maria. David lives in Concord N. H., he mar. Maria Lewis of Boston. They had one dau. Sarah M. Mary A. only dau of Dea. John, mar. David K. Montgomery of Strafford, chil were John S. and David M.

Elizabeth Winkley dau. of Samuel(3) mar. Elmond Layn of Lee. Their chil. were Samuel, John, Mary, Susan, Edmond and David. Benjamin Winkley, son of Samuel(3) mar. Elizabeth Pitman of Barnstead where they lived. They had chil., Sarah b. 22 Aug. 1796, mar. James Leighton of Strafford, Samuel(8) b. Nov. 1799, mar. Mary Martin. They had two sons Jefferson and Alonso, Benjamin jr., b. Feb. 1800, mar. Eliza Holt. Mehitable b. 24 June 1802 mar. Capt. John Felker of Barrington. Their chil. were Isaac G. mar. 1st Hannah A. Hodgdon, 2d Mary V. Young of Madbury. Sarah J. who mar. Horace K. Ford of Dover, Elizabeth mar. John Foss of Rye, Wm. H. mar. Deborah Demeritt of Rochester, Mary S. mar. Joan. F. Berry of Barrington, John W. mar. Mary J. Page of Rochester, Benj. F., Charles Freeman, Augustus A. and Rozanna A. are not mar.—

Eben P. Winkley son of Benjamin(1) b. 12 Oct.
1804, mar. Eliza Whitcomb, Francis(7) b. 2 Mar.
1807, mar. Olive Hannsford, Hannah P. b. 10 Aug.
1811, mar. True Mason. Then there was Wm. P.,
David B. and Elisabeth A. also chil. of Benj. (1).
Col. David, son of Samuel(3) mar. Ann dau. of
Richard Hussey. She died 7 Nov. 1848, aged 64.—
They had no chil.
Mary dau. of Samuel(3) mar. Silas Edgerly of
Madbury. They lived in Barnstead. Their chil.
were David, Samuel, Lorrel, Laura, Mary and Me-
hitable.
Francis Winkley(2) son of Francis(1) mar. Mar-
tha dau. of Mark Hunkling of Barrington. She
was born 1734, d. 16 Jan. 1807. They lived in B.
Their chil. were Mark H. b. 28 Oct. 1763, d. 28
Oct. 1842. Mary wife of Wm. Winkley(2) b. 13
Feb. 1766, d. 0 Oct. 1835. John(4) b. 8 Oct.1769;
d. 8 April 1859, Martha b. 16 May 1771, d. 18
June 1859, Francis b. 1774, d. April 1855, Sarah
b. 1776, died at Barrington 28 August 1845 not
mar.
Mark H. son of Francis(2) mar. Tamson dau. of
Paul Hayes, Esq., of Alton. Their chil were Mercy who mar Isaac Folsom of Alton, they live in
the State of N. Y., Francis(6) mar. Sarah Lougee
of Strafford, Martha mar John Perkins, Esq., of S.,
Paul mar. Lydia Jones of S. and Dennis mar. Ma-
ry A. Howard also of S.
John Winkley(4) son of Francis(2) mar. Ruth
dau. of Stephen Foye. They lived in Barrington.
Their chil. were Asa who mar. Hannah Wingate of
Madbury, Martha mar. Col. Wm. Stearns of Deer-
field. They live in Portsmouth. John H. jr., mar.
1st Kezia Brock also of Barrington, 2d Susan
Brock also of B. Jeremah mar. Maria Langley of
Lee, Wm. P. mar Pamella Crane.
Martha dau. of Francis(2) mar. Shadrach Drew
of Durham. Their chil. were Nicholas, who mar.
Eliza Chesley of Durham, Jeremiah who mar.
Clarissa Nute of Dover, Shadrach mar. Sarah Batch-
eldor of Exeter, Lucinda mar. George Hurd of Ro-
chester. They live in Lowell. Nancy and Sarah
A. died 1831, not mar.
Francis(5) son of Francis(2) mar. Sarah Drew
of Alton., She died 20 March 1846, aged
68. Their chil. were John H. b. 8 Feb. 1800 mar.
Eliza Choate, George b. 10 Mar. 1802, mar. Tam-
son Staunton, Tamson D. b. 4 Aug. 1804, not mar.,
Darius b. 17 June 1807, mar 1st Ursula Hall, 2d
Maria Daniels, 3d Sarah Oats, Cyrus b. 30 Nov.
1809, not mar., Martha M. b. 8 May 1812, mar.
H. F. Whipple, Joseph b. June 1814, mar. Mary
Oater, Abbie b. 22d Jan. 1817, not mar., Francis
M. b. 9 June 1821, mar. Sarah A. Berry.
    We find that the Winkleys as a family have not
been very prolific. The increase as far as we can
ascertain has been but 186 in a period of 182 years,
quite a number have died unmarried, and some
who married left to children. Of the increase 102
were males and 84 females. This record does not
include the number of those who married out of the
name.

WINKLEY FAMILY

BIBLIOGRAPHY

ENGLAND:

1. Devon Parish Registers Read, County Record
   Office, Exeter, Devon, England:

Dawlish, St. Gregory	Woodbury
Sheldon St. Nicholas	Ashcombe
Withcombe Raleigh	Mamhead
St. Thomas by Exeter	Colaton Raleigh
Stoke In Teignhead	Bishopsteignton
Combe in Teignhead	

2. Howard, A.J., The Devon Protestation
   Records, [1641], Bristol England (1973)

3. Howard, A.J., The Devon Muster Roll of
   1569, Bristol, England (1972).

4. Stoate, T.L., Devon Lay Subsidy Rolls
   1524-7, Bristol, England (1979).

5. Devon & Cornwall Record Society, New Series,
   v. 33, p. 38-9 South Devon 1619 Duke of
   Buckingham Survey of mariners & Ships.

6. Index to Manorial court Records at Devon
   Record Office.   [1526631]

7. Stoate, T.L., Devon Hearth Tax Return Lady
   Day 1674, Bristol, England (1982)

8. Oppenheim, M.M., The Maritime History of
   Devon, Exeter, (1968).

9. Rowe, Margary M., Exeter Freemen 1266-1967,
   Devon & Cornwall Record Society, Extra
   Series #1, Exeter (1977)

10. Winkley, Wm Jr., Documents relating to
    Winkley family, Harrow Press, England
    (1863).

11. Cresswell, B.T., The Estuary of the Exe,
    (1902).

BIBLIOGRAPHY Cont.

12. Marriage Licenses 1523 - 1762 Diocese of
    Exeter, Devon Morman Film #0916997 &
    0916980.

13. Misc. County Records at Record Office,
    Exeter, England:

    Dawlish Church Warden Accounts 1588 - 1628.
    Calender of Devon Deeds Quarter Sessions.
    Devon Lay Subsidy Roll 1543/7, 1581 & 1624.
    Devon Hearth Tax List 1664.
    Burnet Morris Card Index, Medievel Devon
      Records.
    Index to Devon Record Office Deeds before
      1840.
    Fursdon's Devon Md. Licenses 1523-1700.
    Dawlish Church Wardens Acc'ts. 1686-1713.
    Dawlish Overseers of the Poor Acc'ts 1667-
      1713.
    1668 Md. License Nicholas Winkley & Mary
      Fryer at St. George by Exeter.

NEW ENGLAND:

Major Sources:

1. Dover Enquirer, 1 May 1862, Winkley Family.
   Author not given.

2. Jesch, Lillian Winkley, <u>Magnificent Men, A
   Winkley Generation</u>, (1966).

3. Goodman, Delmar Winkley, <u>A Winkley Genealogy</u>
   Hanover, NH (1990)

4. Orange Co., Calif., Geneal. Soc. Qty, v. 2,
   #1, p. 6, March 1965, <u>Winkley Genealogy</u>, by
   Lillian W. Jesch.

5. Winkley, Elizabeth L., <u>Winkley Genealogy</u>,
   (1966) Manuscript at NEHGS Library, Boston.

6. Winkley, Nora R., <u>All Our Yesterdays</u>,
   Haywood, Wisc. (1982).

Bibliography Cont.,

7. Noyes, Sybil, <u>Geneal. Dict. of Me. &</u>
   <u>NH</u>, p. 764 (1972).

8. Stearns, E.S., <u>Gen. & Family Hist. of NH</u>,
   p. 1132 (1908).

Other Sources:

1. Collections of the Dover, NH Hist. Soc.,
   Printed by Scales & Quimby, Dover (1894).

2. Graveyards of Barrington, NH, Barr. Hist.
   Soc., p. 24, 79, 88-9 (1976)

3. Hatchett, Frank W., Portsmouth, NH Earliest
   Town Book, 1645-1656, P. 41 (1886)

4. NEHGR: v. 27:271; 79:263; 81:302, 437;
   87:290-1; 125:95.

5. NH Geneal. Record, v.1:98, 161; 3:46-7, 94;
   5:38, 42, 151; 6:160, 173.

6. Saltonstall, Wm G., Ports of Piscataqua,
   (1941).

7. Stakepole, Everett S., Old Kittery & Her
   Families, p. 802-3 (1903).

8. Portsmouth Town Records, Morman Film
   #0015284.

9. Detroit Soc. for Geneal. Research, v. 30,
   #3, p. 20, Fall 1966, "John Winkley of
   Mass."

10. Brewster, C.W., Rambles Around Portsmouth,
    2 vols., p. 2, 59, 99 (1869-1873).

11. ibit, Rambles around Portsmouth, 2nd
    Series.

Bibliography Cont.,

12. Hannah, Priscilla, Gravestone Inscriptions from the Old North Cemetery, Concord, NH 1730-1934, p. 76 (1934)

13. Barnstead Gravestones, v. 6, Morman Film # 0015553.

14. Lowell, Mass. Vital Statistics to 1850, p. 317, 396, 424-5 (   ).

15. Geneal. Records of Durham, NH vol. 1:151.

16. Scales, John , History of Strafford County, NH, Chicago (1914)

17. Early History of Boston Marriages 1700-1809, p. 26, 32, 356, 403 (1903)

18. McDuffee, Franklin, History of the Town of Rochester, NH 1772-1800, 2 v. (1892)

19. Dover Hist. Coll., Dover Hist. Soc., p. 79, 81, 185, 232, 238, 240. (1894).

20. Bouton, Nathaniel, History of Concord, NH, p. 450 (1856).

21. Stackpole, Eevert S., History of the Town of Durham, NH, 2 v. (1913)

22. Hurd, D.H., Rockingham & Strafford Co., NH, p. 707-8 (1882).

23. Hazlett, Chas. A., History of Rockingham Co., NH, Chicago (1915)

24. Epsom, NH Town Report 1937, deaths.

25. NH State Papers, v. 14, 15:299.

27. Biog. Review of York Co., Me. Biog, Review Publ. Co. (1896)

28. DAR Lineage Books: 147:249; 155:203.

29. Mumsell, Frank, American Ancestry, v. 5.
    Albany (1890)
30. So. Church of Portsmouth, NH.

31. US Census, 1790 - 1860.

32. Cook Co., Ill. Death Cert. #14,334-17.

FINAL THOUGHTS

Was the Samuel Winkley who appeared at Portsmouth, NH in 1680 the same individual baptized 1 Oct. 1660 at Dawlish St. Gregory, England? Records found in Co. Devon by Michael J.L. Wickes, AGRA of Bideford, England prove that he was the same person. Let's review the evidence which is quite conclusive.

Nicholas Winkley, the father of the Samuel bp 1 Oct. 1660 at Dawlish, was shown to have been at Portsmouth, NH in 1662. He witnessed the will of Richard Seward Sr. His signature as a witness agrees fully with his signature on the 1669 marriage license at Exeter, England. We know that he was a "mariner." Possible the ships captain of the Properouse owned by Richard Seward.

The names used by Samuel Winkley for his sons is a clue to his father's name. He named his first son for himself. The second was named for his father-in-law. The third son was named NICHOLAS. Was this his fathers name? The Samuel Winkley baptized in 1660 was the son of NICHOLAS WINKLEY.

The parish records for Dawlish and the adjacent parishes do not contain any early death, any marriage nor bapt. of probable children for the SAMUEL WINKLEY who was baptized at Dawlish in 1660. This indicates that he had left the area. It was because he immigrated to Portsmouth, NH in 1680. That is why no later record of his name occurred until after the death of Nicholas in 1687. He is then named as an absentee landlord in the church tax records till 1711. He could have returned to England on occasion.

Why did SAMUEL WINKLEY go first to Portsmouth, NH as a 20 year old man? Did he go to Portsmouth because he knew people there? If so who were these people? Was it the Seward family? In 1662/3 NICHOLAS WINKLEY was associated with them and witnessed the will of RICHARD SEWARD Sr. He may have sent him there to enter the boat

FINAL THOUGHTS Cont.

building trade. SAMUEL WINKLEY was certainly in
the same line of work as was the Seward family.

A review of records for Dawlish and for the
other River Exe Estuary ports was made by
Michael J.L. Wickes of Bideford, England. What
he found showed that the Winkley's of Dawlish
were mariners by profession. The earliest named
was Thomas in 1619. We know that many fishing
vessels from Dawlish sailed to Newfoundland by
1619 to fish. This shows a positive connection
with America from Dawlish at an early date. So
it is quite probable that NICHOLAS WINKLEY of
Dawlish sailed to New England on a regularly
basis.

Association between the Winkley's and the
Seward families at Portsmouth/Kittery continued
for several generations. Both families lived on
Crooked Lane in Kittery. Both were early land
owners at Barrington, etc.

The Seward name is found in County Devon in
the Dawlish area. The author briefly searched
the Co. Devon parish records for the bapt of
Richard Seward Sr. Perhaps the Richard Seaward
who died in 1663 was the Richard s/o Richard
Seaward baptized 16 Jan. 1606 at Heavitree in
Co. Devon. Heavitree parish is adjacent to the
City of Exeter at the head of the River Exe
Estuary. Further research would be needed to
confirm this possibility.

                                        W.H.J.

No.	Name	Birth	No.	Name	Birth
494	Abby A.	1839	600	Charles Edw.	1869
508	Abbie J.	1856	551	Charles E.	1873
241	Abbie P.	1833	1070	Charles E. Jr.	1905
192	Abbie V.	1844	288	Charles F.	1854
192	Abbie V.	1844	1006	Charles H.	1886
86	Abiah	1806	327	Charles P.	1849
287	Abiel Clinton	___	1200	Charles T.	c1894
187	Abigail A.	c1818	1223	Charles V.	1913
142	Abigail H.	1817	314	Charles W.	1858
352	Abraham	1834	75	Charlotte C.	1807
610	Ada Ohio	___	1072	Charlotte	1915
271	Ada W.	c1858	506	Chrystine M.	1853
253	Adeline	1827	328	Clara	1851
535	Albert	___	76	Clarissa	___
1051	Albert Mark	1889	257	Clarisse	1839
532	Alice Maud	1876	354	Clark	1840
282	Alma L.L.	1842	139	Cyrus	1809
206	Alonzo	___	313	Cyrus A.	1853
197	Alonzo K.	c1822			
580	Alta G.	1873			
570	Alton Bunford	1877	504	Daniel S.	1845
1022	Amy	1899	195	Daniel Swain	___
331	Andrew S.	1848	100	Daniel	1792
94	Ann	1796	138	Darius	1807
343	Anna	1846	310	Darius D.	1847
356	Anne	1847	48	David, Col.	1775
280	Artemisia C.	1836	104	David	c1810
130	Asa	1801	182	David	___
284	Atazine M.	1847	1070i	David	___
			115	David B.	1821
			188	David B.	1822
			304	David C.	1847
611	Bada A.	___	124	Dennis	1808
185	Benjamin F.	1816	36	Dorcus	1782
1003	Benjamin F.	1877	38	Dorothy	
47	Benjamin M.	1772	1020	Dorothy	1904
108	Benjamin Jr.	1800			
264	Betsy	c1839			
			110	Ebenezer P.	1804
			213	Eben P.	1857
			330	Edson S.	1835
292	Charles	1834	507	Elisa J.	1853
1030	Charles	1893	258	Eliza J.	c1846
213	Charles E.	1857	9	Elizabeth	c1703

No.	Name	Birth
12	Elizabeth	1728
19	Elizabeth	___
33	Elizabeth/Lydia	___
46	Elizabeth	1769
81	Elizabeth	1783
114	Elizabeth Ann	1819
308	Elizabeth R.	1858
269	Ella T.	1851
267	Ellen F.	c1846
16	Emerson	1740
261	Emily H.	c1833
536	Emma	___
273	Emma E.	c1862
242	Emma Lougee	___
88	Enoch	c1782
1201	Ernest L.	c1896
1050	Erwin Mark	1885
344	Esal	1850
37	Esther	___
1202	Ethel May	1901
531	Evelyn May	1872
540	Flora	1839
545	Flora Idella	1859
302	Florance	___
244n	Florette E.	___
1005i	Forrest	___
3	Francis	1689
14	Francis	1733
42	Francis	1759
31	Francis	1765
54	Francis	1774
121	Francis	1797
111	Francis	1803
537	Francis/Frank	1864
178	Francis John	1830
154	Francis L.	1825
143	Francis M.	1821
276	Francis S.	1832
539	Frank	1855
1003	Frank B.	1877
537	Frank Chowen	1864
307	Frank D.	1855
530	Frank H.	1868

No.	Name	Birth
1026	Frank Jr.	1908
533	G. Edward	1875
1029	Genevieve	1916
260	George	c1831
294	George	1840
303	George C.	1851
577	George Langdon	1879
136	George W.	1802
211	George Wash.	1846
575	Grace Ellen	1873
543	Hannah Amanda	1855
112	Hannah P.	1811
612	Harriet V.	1850
1215	Harry A.	c1901
1023	Harry Francis	1887
1224	Harry Francis	1915
1025	Hazel	1896
353	Helen	1838
1061	Helen	1910
96	Henry	1803
268	Herbert C.	1849
1005	Hiram A.	1882
189	Holman R.	1824
96	Hunking	1803
547	Ida May	1863
1050	Irving Mark	1885
301	Isabel	1845
538	Isora E.	1849
342	James	1845
73	James Folsom	1802
1225	Jane Elizabeth	1923
270	Jason W.	c1856
205	Jefferson M.	___
133	Jeremiah	1807
275	Jeremiah Otis	1830
196	Jeremiah S.	1816
1004	Jeremiah S.	1879

No.	Name	Birth
105	Mary A.	___
198	Mary A.	___
199	Mary A.	___
221	Mary A.	___
152	Mary Ann	1815
510	Mary Ann	1860
74	Mary Ann F.	1804
266	Mary E.	c1844
191	Mary E.	1840
272	Mary E.	c1860
321	Mary F.	c1844
497	Mary G.	1846
176	Mary S.	1816
120	Mary/Mercy	1792
43	Mehitable	1761
83	Mehitable	1789
109	Mehitable	1802
281	Melville L.	1837
262	Mercy	1835
6	Michael	1699
1	Nicholas	c1610
5	Nicholas	1694
1024	Nora M.	1891
1221	Nora Marian	1911
351	Olean	1833
84	Olive	___
220	Olive F.	1849
295	Oren	1842
193	Otis Plummer	1816
123	Paul	1803
548	Paul Edgar	1865
256	Paul Hayes Jr.	1835
550	Paul Herman	1874
90	Paul T.	1786
183	Paul T.	1810
499	Paul T.	___
242	Rebecca Lougee	___

No.	Name	Birth
340	Richard	1840
1220	Robert Francis	1909
1007	Roscoe Elmer	1889
1	Samuel	1660
2	Samuel	1687
10	Samuel	1721
13	Samuel	1730/1
41	Samuel Jr.	1756
85	Samuel	c1796
87	Samuel	___
107	Samuel	1797
97	Samuel	1805
102	Samuel	___
160	Samuel Hobart	1819
4	Sarah	___
17	Sarah	1741
18	Sarah	___
35	Sarah	___
55	Sarah	1776
95	Sarah	1798
106	Sarah	1795
212	Sarah Eliz.	1852
542	Sarah Frances	1854
341	Sarah J.	1841
177	Sarah L.	1818
201	Sarah M.	c1835
305	Sarah M.	1849
495	Sarah Maria	1842
555	Sarah Tilton	1881
501	Stephen O.	1838
1216	Steve Clark	___
350	Susan	1831
89	Swain	___
103	Swain	1802
137	Tamson D.	1804
240	Tamson Hayes	1824
326	Thomas Benton	1847
311	Ursula Maria	1851

No.	Name	Birth
1071	Vera	1908
498	Viola Frances	1848
578	Williard Choate	1885
7	William	1700
20	William	1739
44	William	1763
72	William	____
150	William	1807
1031	William	1902
1062	William	1916
303	William C.	1847
60	William K.	1766
186	William M. J.	1815
251	William M.	1824
91	William M. Jr.	1789
244	William Pitt	1829
134	William P.	____
113	William Plummer	1816
210	William Warren	1839
1021	Wilma	1889
1027	Winifred	1913

Name	Anc, No,
Yeaton, Alfred D.	531
Doris	531ii
Gladys	531i
Margaret	531iii
Young, Ellen Sarah	300
Mary	43
Polly	132

Heritage Books by William Haslet Jones:

CD: *Genealogies, Volume 6: The William Haslet Jones Collection*

*Philip Towle, Hampton, New Hampshire: His English Origins
and Some American Descendants*

*The Rowell Family of New England and Their English Origins, 1560–1900:
Descendants of Thomas Rowell 1594–1662*

Vital Statistics of Chichester, New Hampshire, 1742–1927

Vital Statistics of Epsom, New Hampshire, 1727–1927

Vital Statistics of North Hampton, New Hampshire, 1742–1942

Vital Statistics of Seabrook, New Hampshire, 1768–1903

William Tilton: His English Origins and Some American Descendants

*Winkley Family: The English Origin of Captain Samuel Winkley
and Some New England Descendants*

The Yeaton Family of New England, 1650–1900